"In the Old Testament, when it came to [...] God always
had a man in mind to lead the way. Ha[...]
Daniel Henderson, it may well be he is [...]
helping to set the stage for true spiritual [...]

—Joni Eareckson Tada, Joni and Fri[...]

"As a pastor for over two decades, Daniel Henderson was passionate about
helping churches experience authentic renewal. Today, as a pastor to pastors,
Daniel inspires leaders to renewed courage and impact. Now, in *The Deeper
Life*, he writes once again to help you with a unique and practical plan for
spiritual authenticity. In a world of constant distraction and chronic discouragement, this book offers strategic focus and hope for the daily journey."

—Mark Batterson, *New York Times* bestselling author
of *The Circle Maker*

"I am not much of a theologian, but after reading through the pages of
Daniel Henderson's book, I feel I am more of one than ever before. It was
that thought-provoking. . . . Read it!"

—H.B. London, president of H.B. London Ministries;
pastor to pastors emeritus for Focus on the Family

"Whatever habits or failures or strongholds keep you from realizing who
you are in Christ, you can put them behind you and experience freedom
and joy. . . . If you're searching for personal fulfillment or looking for
guidance through difficult challenges, Henderson's practical and insightful
book is just what you need."

—Cheryl Sacks, author of *The Prayer Saturated Church*;
co-founder of BridgeBuilders Int'l Leadership Network

"Daniel Henderson has not only been a mentor to me, I've watched him
invest in thousands of young leaders. His commitment to fostering spiritual renewal in the church is fueling the faith of generations."

—Johnnie Moore, author of *Dirty God*;
vice president of Liberty University

"In the cacophony and chaos of life, Daniel Henderson powerfully reminds
us of the deep, daily spiritual disciplines God uses to renew us. Like a
rudder to our souls, he directs us away from the mindless activity to the
meaningful choices that can mark us well for our Savior."

—Paul Nyquist, PhD, president of Moody Bible Institute

"Instead of skimming our way through the hectic pace of our lives, this
book is a refreshing pause that motivates us to ask the deeper questions
about why we do what we do. I commend Daniel's approach to an integrated life and his innovative daily plan for personal renewal."

—Hans Finzel, founder of HDLeaders.com;
author of *The Top Ten Mistakes Leaders Make*

"Daniel Henderson knows the deeper Christian life, because he has lived it for over twenty-five years. All who read this book have a great mentor and will grow as they respond to his admonitions."

—Elmer Towns, co-founder of Liberty University

"This unique book will encourage every Christian who aspires to be effective in fulfilling God's distinctive calling and purpose."

—Luis Bush, international facilitator for Transform World Connections; architect of the 10/40 and 4/14 Windows

"Daniel Henderson has his finger on the pulse of Christians who are saved and growing spiritually but who are missing the connections between their theology and an actual life of joy and purpose. . . . Without being programmatic or too tactical, Henderson provides a sound process for people to live the life God originally intended them to live."

—Jeff Spadafora, director of global coaching services for Halftime

"Daniel's thirst for authentic intimacy with Christ is contagious. *The Deeper Life* couldn't be more timely for a generation desperately seeking God."

—Tim Clinton, president of the American Association of Christian Counselors

"Daniel Henderson is a man of deep and consistent faith, purpose, and prayer. He lives out everything he writes about, so . . . if you want to unleash the longings of your soul, you'd better read this book!"

—Karen and Jim Covell, founding directors of the Hollywood Prayer Network

"Daniel Henderson's passion to see spiritual renewal in churches and in the lives of believers is challenging and contagious. I believe this book is a true gift to the church and is going to impact people all over the world."

—Brian Bloye, senior pastor of West Ridge Church, Dallas, GA; co-author of *It's Personal*

"Daniel's ministry is extremely refreshing as he communicates in a down-to-earth way about the questions and issues that we all face in our Christian walk. He makes it plain—equipping readers with practical how-tos for transforming their spiritual journeys."

—Chrissy Cymbala Toledo, worship leader, The Chicago Tabernacle

"In over thirty years of pastoral ministry, I have never been more impacted spiritually, or more excited personally, about the work God is doing through Daniel Henderson and the ministry of Strategic Renewal. This book is an essential part of that work, and everyone who reads it will be more than glad they did."

—Danny Hodges, senior pastor of Calvary Chapel, St. Petersburg, FL

THE
DEEPER
LIFE

SATISFYING THE
8 VITAL LONGINGS
OF YOUR SOUL

DANIEL HENDERSON
WITH BRENDA BROWN

BETHANYHOUSE
a division of Baker Publishing Group
Minneapolis, Minnesota

Published by Bethany House Publishers
11400 Hampshire Avenue South
Bloomington, Minnesota 55438
www.bethanyhouse.com

Bethany House Publishers is a division of
Baker Publishing Group, Grand Rapids, Michigan

Printed in the United States of America

Library of Congress Cataloging-in-Publication Data
Henderson, Daniel.
     The deeper life : satisfying the 8 vital longings of your soul / Daniel Henderson.
        pages   cm.
     Includes bibliographical references.
     Summary: "Author and ministry leader Daniel Henderson shows readers how
to live out their long-term spiritual goals through a step-by-step guide to daily
renewal"—Provided by publisher.
     ISBN 978-0-7642-1177-5 (pbk. : alk. paper)1. Christian life. I. Title.
BV4501.3.H448 2014
248—dc23   2013039150

Emphasis in Scripture shown by italics is the author's.

Unless otherwise indicated, Scripture quotations are from the New King James Version. Copyright © 1982 by Thomas Nelson, Inc. Used by permission. All rights reserved.

Scripture quotations identified NASB are from the New American Standard Bible®, copyright © 1960, 1962, 1963, 1968, 1971, 1972, 1973, 1975, 1977, 1995 by The Lockman Foundation. Used by permission.

Scripture quotations identified MESSAGE are from *The Message* by Eugene H. Peterson, copyright © 1993, 1994, 1995, 2000, 2001, 2002. Used by permission of NavPress Publishing Group. All rights reserved.

Scripture quotations identified ESV are from The Holy Bible, English Standard Version® (ESV®), copyright © 2001 by Crossway, a publishing ministry of Good News Publishers. Used by permission. All rights reserved. ESV Text Edition: 2007

Scripture quotations marked NLT are from the *Holy Bible*, New Living Translation, copyright © 1996, 2004, 2007 by Tyndale House Foundation. Used by permission of Tyndale House Publishers, Inc., Carol Stream, Illinois 60188. All rights reserved.

Scripture quotations identified TLB are from *The Living Bible*, copyright © 1971. Used by permission of Tyndale House Publishers, Inc., Wheaton, Illinois 60189. All rights reserved.

Scripture quotations identified AMP are from the Amplified® Bible, copyright © 1954, 1958, 1962, 1964, 1965, 1987 by The Lockman Foundation. Used by permission.

Scripture quotations marked KJV are from the King James Version of the Bible.

Cover design by Lookout Design, Inc.

14   15   16   17   18   19   20   7   6   5   4   3   2   1

To my son, Jordan David Henderson,
whose passion to worship God
has become the foundation and fuel
for his godly example as a Christ-follower,
husband, and father.

Books by
Daniel Henderson

FROM BETHANY HOUSE PUBLISHERS

Transforming Prayer
The Deeper Life

Contents

Contents

Foreword

My friend Daniel Henderson is a man on a mission. In recent years, he and I have been honored to minister together in one-day events in cities across North America, encouraging pastors in their calling to serve Christ and His church. The Lord has helped Daniel to be a blessing to these church leaders and to equip them to lead spiritual renewal in their congregations.

In 2007 Daniel left the security and familiarity of his role as the senior pastor of a prominent church to step out in faith and give his life to serving the body of Christ for the sake of an awakening of prayer and practical renewal. As I have watched him teach, lead prayer experiences, and serve his fellow leaders, I have been blessed to see God's hand on his life and divine blessing on the vital focus of his ministry.

In this book, Daniel helps believers from every walk of life experience renewal by making specific application of the gospel to daily life. The gospel of Jesus Christ brings us into an accurate and vital understanding of the one true God. It transforms how we see ourselves in this world. It ignites meaningful purpose and guides the way we manage our daily priorities and decisions. The gospel breathes eternal significance into every dimension of our journey. Here, Daniel shows us this reality, in the most practical of terms.

With the goal of a deeper, more thoughtful approach to the Christian life, this book calls us to search God's Word, examine our hearts, and seek the mind of the Holy Spirit for concrete answers to the deep questions of the soul. Drawing from his own life's journey and years of experience in pastoral ministry, Daniel will help men and women, young and old, experience spiritual victory through a life of worship, integrity, and nonconformity to the world.

As Daniel reminds us, we all want to come to the end of this life with the assurance that we have deposited a legacy of spiritual authenticity and eternal significance in the hearts of those who have known us well. I pray you will embrace Daniel's message and engage in this clear path of living a more intentional and fruitful life for the glory of our Lord Jesus Christ.

Pastor Jim Cymbala
The Brooklyn Tabernacle Church

A Deeper Life Story

Tragedy has a way of testing the heart. It also has a way of revealing the truth. Because it's in the chaos of life's tragedies, and how you react to them, that you learn the truth about yourself: what you believe about God, what you believe about yourself, what really matters . . . *life's deepest questions*.

On a spectacular spring afternoon, Greg Haroutunian, his wife, and their three children stood along the finish line of the 2013 Boston Marathon, cheering on a friend who was racing to raise money for cancer research. Eagerly awaiting their friend's approach, they first heard what they thought was a cannon shot celebrating someone crossing the finish line. Seconds later, just fifteen yards away, directly across Boylston Street, a second bomb that had been placed in a pressure cooker exploded and sent the entire city, and country, into panic. In the minutes that followed, Greg's family witnessed front-row carnage, including the tragic death of an eight-year-old boy.

After the fire trucks and rescue teams arrived, the family made its way to the Boston subway. Rounding a corner, Greg spied a trash can on the street and understandably thought that it too could contain a bomb. Shielding his family as they passed by, he was suddenly overwhelmed with the assurance that their lives were in God's hands.

The hours and days to follow were extremely tense for Greg and his family. We spoke on the phone one afternoon while their neighborhood was on lockdown as police went door to door looking for the remaining suspect who had orchestrated the crime.

Thankfully, in the months preceding this tragic experience, Greg had been part of a pastors' group I was leading through a process of clarifying some of the core questions of the soul. He had taken the time to write out his own personal theology statement. Reviewing the Scriptures he had memorized from his days with The Navigators and some of his favorite books on the character of God, Greg had written and memorized his answers to life's greatest questions.

And, on the afternoon after the bombing, Greg leaned heavily on these declarations, affirming himself again and again with what he had written:

- God is unchanging, good, faithful, holy, sovereign, almighty, gracious, condescending, merciful, loving, righteous, kind, the Father, the Lord, communicative, and worthy.
- Therefore, He will care for me, keep His promises, reveal himself, accomplish His desires, guard me, allow difficulties and trials, never give me more than I can bear, mold me into Christ's likeness.
- So, I will rest, trust, sacrifice, live with abandon, full tilt, be unashamed, confident, not self-conscious, cling to hope, embrace my humanity/weaknesses, care for others, never stop learning, growing, seeking to know more and express more of our awesome God to anyone who will listen.

Today, Greg recounts, "Having these realities memorized made the truth accessible. I was refreshed, rejuvenated, and lifted. The world literally blew up right in front of my face. But God did not blow up. . . . This very concrete, practical engagement with God's character through this process assured me that I was absolutely invincible until the Lord calls me home."

Greg has also articulated a biblical identity statement along with his written life purpose statement. He meditates on these truths each evening as he falls asleep and each morning as he awakens. "This whole process has been so empowering. It anchors me as I fade into sleep and gives me deep enthusiasm to start the day. I am able to find purpose in the midst of the chaos.

"Had I not gone through this exercise, it would have all been too big for me in the moment—too hard to try and gather some truth to hold onto. But it was immediately available when I needed it. Moments like these will come for all of us. For most people, it probably will not be a bomb. But in some way, we will all face times when we need God's truth close at hand."

Introduction

Men for the sake of getting a living forget to live.
—*Margaret Fuller*

The hardest thing about the Christian life is that
it is so *daily*.

The Musée Rodin in Paris, France, is dedicated to the works of the French sculptor Auguste Rodin. The displays include 6,600 sculptures, 16,000 drawings and photographs, and 7,000 other objects of art. Each year, 700,000 visitors frequent the collection.

Probably most famous of all Rodin's creations is *The Thinker*. First cast in 1880, this bronze figure of a nude man sits atop a marble pedestal. Hand on his chin, looking down, he seems to ponder. And we wonder, *What is he thinking about?* My first thought is that he must be working hard to remember where he left his clothes. In reality, he simply represents the journey of all earth travelers. As the book of Job notes, we came into the world naked, and naked we will return. Stripped of all the superficial trappings of life, we are left with our thoughts and looking for answers.

The truth is we were created to think deeply about something more than meets the eye in this life. The Bible says God has placed eternity in our hearts (Ecclesiastes 3:11), compelling us to yearn for conclusions that will satisfy the soul. We were made to ask questions, to discover meaning beyond mere physical existence. Thus begins the quest.

The deep longings of our soul drive us to ask questions and seek answers, but rarely do we arrive at any sound conclusions. We search through the latest smartphone apps and download e-books on self-improvement. We scroll through posts and pins looking for inspiration, then repeat and re-tweet the insights of others. We increasingly look to the "cloud" to organize and simplify our lives. Still, most of us crawl into bed each night with a feeling that something is missing. Too often, it is.

We all yearn for a compelling mission in life. If only we could figure out what it is supposed to be! We feel the need to be guided by a clear set of values and long to leave a lasting legacy, but lose our way in the fog of daily distractions. Disoriented, we don't know which direction to go. Knowing that any mediocre road will take us to nowhere in particular, we feel the pressure to choose the best direction. We just aren't sure how to make a wise selection for a rewarding destination. Paralyzed and perplexed, we falter in our forward progress.

The demands of work, home, family, church, and society leave us feeling overwhelmed. Each night our to-do list remains full of undone tasks. As we doze off to sleep, we feel this haunting sense that we will never get on top of things. When the alarm goes off the next morning, we shower, eat, and rush out the door, saying to ourselves, *I've got to get going.* Perhaps we would do well to ask, *Where am I going?* and *Why am I in such a hurry to get there?* followed by *How's this working for me?*

Deep or Wide?

A tree's root system is vital to its growth. It takes in and transports water and minerals from the soil to the rest of the tree. Depending on water and soil conditions, roots can grow as deep as twenty feet, providing a firm anchor for the tree above ground. The growth of the roots, however, can be restricted by soil compaction—a reduction in air pockets resulting from soil particles being packed together. Like a barely rooted tree, our lives are becoming more compacted every day by the countless options and mental traffic of modern life. The "air" of meaningful reflection and intentional living seems to grow more and more scarce. We want and need to go deeper for our own soul satisfaction and positive influence on others, but need help in doing so.

In our world where well over 100 million apps are downloaded every year,[1] we are confronted with options, ads, and invitations beyond human ability to fully grasp or comprehend, let alone keep up. We have become the consummate society of multitaskers and it's apparently remapping our brains. One Stanford University professor concludes, "The neural circuits devoted to scanning, skimming, and multitasking are expanding and strengthening, while those used for reading and thinking deeply, with sustained concentration, are weakening or eroding." He notes, "We have become suckers for irrelevancy."[2]

A friend of mine asked for prayer recently, stating that "the devil is always launching weapons of mass distraction on my life."

When we lack direction and are bombarded by distractions we become discouraged. I define discouragement as a temporary loss of perspective. As Margaret Fuller observed, "Men for the sake of getting a living forget to live." Each day is significant in the pursuit of a deeper life. It must be seized with a renewal that maintains our perspective and minimizes the distractions that afflict us.

Our physical body can soon become ill without proper care and nutrition. A marriage can become troubled after just a few episodes of unresolved anger and misunderstanding. An automobile can break down without proper maintenance. So can our lives become uprooted as a result of shallow living, without daily guidance and renewal in God's presence.

In the busyness of adapting to the daily demands and orders of a noisy world, we've forgotten that God has a plan for us to win the daily battle. He wants us to sink roots deep into the soil of His promises and allow His truth to be absorbed into the core of our soul.

The Contest of Our Lives

In our quest for fulfillment, we must remember this life is not a leisurely stroll through the meadow. Paul described the Christian life as an athletic competition in which we run, wrestle, strive, and compete. Key New Testament passages use warfare terminology relevant to every life and generation (e.g., Romans 13:12–14; Ephesians 6:10–13; 2 Corinthians 2:14; 2 Timothy 2:4). We are compelled to remain combat ready, mentally prepared, and equipped to win the contest.

The battlefronts are not obscure, and our primary enemies are not clandestine. We are struggling against the devil, our own sinful flesh, and the depraved world system in which we live. All three forces conspire to defeat us. Yet we are destined to triumph when "the weapons of our warfare are not carnal but mighty in God for pulling down strongholds," consistently and strategically (see 2 Corinthians 10:1–6).

Much is at stake. Real satisfaction and ultimate significance hang in the balance. Our personal spiritual survival, the health of our relationships, the well-being of our families, and the destiny of our earthly journey compel us to know how to win the daily battle. I fear most of us feel like we are losing. Sadly, we are not sure why or what to do about it. Thankfully, it doesn't have to be that way.

A Life Plan for an Everyday Win

You are holding in your hand a guide for your daily "win." It is a win that matters and a victory that is biblical. The process is proven. But like anything of value, you will have to work for it. Dig in, because the effort will be well worth it.

Three ideals frame meaning and victory for each of us as we confront the devil, the flesh, and the world:

Worship + Integrity + Nonconformity = **WIN**

Worship is the ultimate foundation and passion that overcomes the devil. Integrity is the commitment that provides victory over the flesh. Nonconformity is our triumphant, transcendent response to the temptations and trials of a fallen world.

Worship: The FUEL for a Deeper Life

Worship begins with a biblical and ultimately practical understanding of the character of God. It results in a life of wholehearted surrender and sacrifice. I define worship as "the response of all I am to the revelation of all God is."

Winning against the wiles of the devil is rooted in pure, passionate worship. When confronting Satan's attacks in the wilderness, Jesus announced, "Away with you, Satan! For it is written, 'You shall worship the LORD your God, and Him only you shall serve'" (Matthew 4:10). To win our daily battle, we must be clothed in the person and provision of Jesus Christ the Son of God. We must utilize the sword of the Spirit, which is the announcement of the truth of God's Word. This is a declaration and application of the truth of the purpose and plan of God. It is the overflow of worship.

As you may have surmised by the table of contents, I want to guide you in answering eight essential questions. Your answers are designed to spark powerful and practical daily renewal. But all eight answers rest squarely on the clarity and conviction of the first issue: worship. This is a worship springing from a biblical and personal response to the first question: "Who is God?"

Integrity: The FIBER of a Deeper Life

We've all seen the lives of people we love and respect unravel. Twice in my pastoral ministry I have followed pastors of large churches who chose moral failure over a fruitful finish. We all wonder how this heartbreaking scenario unfolds.

One primary culprit is compartmentalization. *Merriam-Webster* defines it as "isolation or splitting off of part of the personality or mind with lack of communication and consistency between the parts."[3] Simply put, compartmentalization is the opposite of integrity.

In my favorite psalm, David affirms that the true disciple "walks with integrity, and works righteousness, and speaks truth in his heart" (Psalm 15:2 NASB). This is the picture of a blameless lifestyle. We see a person who always seeks to do the right thing. He is empowered for righteousness because he tells himself the truth in the depths of his being.

For years my life felt like a jigsaw puzzle. I had a handful of interesting and essential pieces. I simply could not make them fit together to complete the picture of what my life should become. In identifying the core issues of my soul and formulating truth that I could speak every day in the depths of my being, the pieces began to connect.

Integrity is a life where all the pieces fit together. We must know the pieces, define them accurately, understand them biblically, and then connect them in a way that makes sense for life. This is the framework of the journey we are about to enjoy.

To do this, we need the wisdom and power of the Holy Spirit. God's Spirit, who lives within our hearts, was repeatedly described by Christ as the "Spirit of truth" (John 14:17; 15:26; 16:13). But our flesh wants to adopt the lies of compartmentalization. We easily resist the penetration of transforming truth into every area of our life—thoroughly and simultaneously. Paul tells us, "Walk in the Spirit, and you shall not fulfill the lust of the flesh. For the flesh lusts against the Spirit, and the Spirit against the flesh" (Galatians 5:16–17). He goes on to describe the massively destructive works of the flesh—all of which are the antithesis of integrity.

As you clarify solidly scriptural and personally applicable truths—about your identity, purpose, values, priorities, goals, and time—the pieces will begin to fit together. This integrity is the framework of a meaningful and winning life plan.

Nonconformity: The FRUIT of a Deeper Life

Anyone familiar with the book of Romans knows that the first eleven chapters are packed with some of the richest theological truth ever written. Paul then transitions with these memorable commands:

> I beseech you therefore, brethren, by the mercies of God, that you present your bodies a living sacrifice, holy, acceptable to God, which is your reasonable service. And do not be conformed to this world,

but be transformed by the renewing of your mind, that you may prove what is that good and acceptable and perfect will of God.

Romans 12:1–2

Nonconformity flows from authentic worship as the fruit of regular transforming renewal. Do you want to live differently? Do you want to discover regular victory in the battle against the devil, the flesh, and the world? Do you want to leave a distinctive and memorable legacy when you cross the finish line of life? You can. A holy, healthy nonconformity is possible and promised. You don't have to just "fit" into the world's fleeting and irrelevant systems.

Wake Up, Renew, Repeat

I have concluded from my own spiritual quest, as well as from shepherding thousands of souls in pastoral ministry, that the hardest thing about the Christian life is that it is so DAILY. The rising sun on our everyday journey brings the opportunity to win or lose in the spiritual contest. The glowing dusk calls out to us to evaluate the real meaning of the day and the eternal value of our efforts.

We live each day not by bread alone but by every word that proceeds from the mouth of God. The fresh manna of spiritual nourishment is perishable and must be consumed in a timely and consistent pursuit. Paul knew that repeated "renewal" in truth must resonate at the core of our daily victory: "Therefore we do not lose heart. Even though our outward man is perishing, yet the inward man is being *renewed day by day*" (2 Corinthians 4:16). Paul nailed it again in Colossians 3:10, encouraging those who "have put on the new man who is *renewed in knowledge* according to the image of Him who created him." Again we land on the core idea of daily renewal in the truths of Christ and who we are in Him.

Eight Longings and the Answers That Shape Your Legacy

This book will guide you to recognize and address the deepest needs and questions of the soul. As you consider the biblical answers and create specific, practical affirmations for daily review in response to these questions, renewal and victory will result.

1. **The Longing**
   To know and experience God in the fullness of His person and presence
   - **The Question:** Who is God?
   - **The Issue:** My theology

2. **The Longing**
   To live from an authentic core of biblical self-understanding and security
   - **The Question:** Who am I?
   - **The Issue:** My identity

3. **The Longing**
   To give one's life to a worthy cause
   - **The Question:** Why am I here?
   - **The Issue:** My purpose

4. **The Longing**
   To be respected as a person of sound principles and solid character
   - **The Question:** What really matters?
   - **The Issue:** My values

5. **The Longing**
   To focus on and fulfill rewarding and meaningful commitments.
   - **The Question:** What shall I do?
   - **The Issue:** My priorities

6. **The Longing**
   To enjoy strategic and effective accomplishment of worthwhile objectives
   - **The Question:** How shall I do it?
   - **The Issue:** My goals

7. **The Longing**
   To be a faithful steward of eternally significant opportunities

- **The Question:** When shall I do it?
- **The Issue:** My time

8. **The Longing**
   To be remembered as a person of extraordinary contribution
   - **The Question:** How will I finish?
   - **The Issue:** My legacy

> *You will discover that your theology is the basis of your identity. Your identity is expressed through a clear purpose. Your purpose is guided by values. Your values determine your priorities. Your priorities are implemented by your goals. Your goals are accomplished by your stewardship of time. And all of this, when understood clearly and embraced daily, results in a legacy that really matters.*

Pearls of Daily Wisdom

In a recent leadership conference, I heard Jim Collins, professor and author of books like *Built to Last* and *Good to Great*, describe his goal as a teacher. He said his job is to offer thought-provoking ideas and to leave people with "grains of sand in their minds." These ideas, mulled over in the mind through contemplation, create an "irritation" that over time become pearls of wisdom.

This book is designed to leave grains of truth in your mind. The questions are designed to be delightfully provoking. And while the answers aren't always easily arrived at, they are clearly worth the energy. Serious consideration of them will invariably form pearls of discovery that will result in your life being more integrated than ever before. The effort and time invested will prove profitable—for now and for eternity.

For fifteen years, most of my mornings have commenced with an essential reiteration of truth about the issues that formulate daily victory. I tell myself the truth about God, my life, and my future by way of a recorded summary of eight answers. The selection on my iPod is well utilized. Whether walking on the treadmill, reflecting during my quiet time, or flying to a speaking engagement, I am able to renew my mind in the truths that matter most.

You may never record your answers for audio review, but I hope you will clarify, write out, and review these essential truths every day. This book will show you how. The approach has worked for me and helped thousands of others. It can work for you too.

The Road to Real Change and Renewal

This passion for renewal began for the apostle Paul one day on a dusty road to a town called Damascus. Let's walk the transformational trail with him for just a moment as we conclude.

He was the classic example of a man climbing the ladder of success only to find that it was leaning against the wrong wall. Everyone in his day knew him as Saul. His eventual name change reflected a true transformation of identity. It all started with an encounter with the living Christ, sparking some agonizing questions, resulting in a pursuit of the right answers, manifested in a life of renewal and legacy of incredible significance.

Saul was a driven man, passionate to get to the top and make for himself a name. On this day, the Jewish zealot was on the road again. He headed north from Jerusalem, hot on the trail of those Christians who had fled his persecuting passion. Saul could not tolerate the people of the Way, who posed a threat to his tightly organized world.

But it all changed in a flash—literally. An inexplicable bright light at midday left him on his face, blind and baffled. In that hour of crisis, he was confronted with the truth about what was wrong with his life and how he needed to change his ways. In the days that followed, he would contemplate answers to the most important questions he had ever asked.

They spilled out in that defining moment as Paul encountered the living Jesus. "Who are You, Lord?" Paul asked. And as naturally as *B* follows *A*, he also inquired, "What do You want me to do?" (Acts 9:5–6).

The answers he discovered made all the difference in his world—just as they will in ours. Today, the reality of Saul's quest is very much like our own. We need an encounter with the living Christ. We need to ask Him for the answers to the questions deep in our soul. Ultimately we want Him to reveal to our hearts the truth of *who* He is and then show us *how* to live. Then we can renew our minds in these conclusions and weave them into the very fabric of our lives.

I pray this book will help you live a deeper life by providing a plan for transformation and triumph—every day.

How to Use This Book

Here are seven keys to getting the most from this book:

- **Read**—As you read, take time to absorb the ideas, making your own notes and praying about the things that speak most directly and powerfully to your heart.

- **Reflect**—Utilize the Discovery Exercises in Part Two to interact more specifically with each question, allowing this thoughtful interaction to pave the way for your own written answers to each question. You can engage in these exercises after each chapter, or wait until you have finished reading the book to begin.

- **Record**—Start writing your answers to each question in words that reflect biblical truth and also directly express the needs and journey of your own life. Trust the Holy Spirit to give you insight and clarity. The idea is that over time you will rewrite and refine your answers.

- **Relate**—Participate with others in the journey. The discussion questions at the end of the book are designed to guide you to meaningful interaction with others as you address biblical answers to the longings of your soul. You can also utilize **The Deeper Life** small-group DVD series, available at www.strategicrenewal.com.

- **Renew**—Begin a daily habit of renewing your mind and heart through the answers you have clarified through this process, with the help of the Holy Spirit. Make this review process a vital part of your daily "WIN." **The Deeper Life Summary** at the back of the book will be a place to review your final answers.

- Realize—Sign up for personal or group coaching in this renewal process so you can realize the full potential of what this book offers and the application of the answers to your deepest longings, making your renewal experience a lifestyle for the glory of God. For more information on the coaching journey centered in these eight questions, go to www.strategicrenewal.com/8QCoaching.

- Reproduce—Perhaps you will feel called to guide others through this dynamic process of daily renewal and life transformation. If you would like to learn more about becoming a part of our "8Q" coaching team, email us at coaching@strategicrenewal.com.

Part One

THE
DEEPER LIFE

Longings, Questions, and Answers

1

Who Is God?

In the beginning God created mankind in His
image, and man has been returning the favor
ever since.

—*Unknown*

God is.
God is near.
God is love,
Longing to communicate himself to me.
God the Almighty One
Who worketh all in all,
Is even now waiting to work in me,
And make himself known.

—*Andrew Murray*

f you were even remotely tuned in to television during the mid-
to late-1990s, you are familiar with America's love affair with
Gidget the dog. She became so popular that she flew first-class,
opened up the New York Stock Exchange, and even made an appearance at Madison Square Garden. Gidget starred in numerous
commercials and transcended the "burger wars," in which several
fast-food chains were actually producing advertisements against
one another. You will remember her as "The Taco Bell Chihuahua"   29

(maybe assuming it was a boy dog). Often dressed in traditional Mexican gear, she spoke using special effects via the professional voice of Carlos Alazraqui. Many of her lines became mainstream to American culture, including "¡Yo quiero Taco Bell!" "Viva Gorditas!" and "Drop the chalupa!"

My personal favorite first appeared in 1998 and features the downtown streets of a large city late at night. Homemade signs point the way to a plate of tacos on the sidewalk. Gidget stands expectantly near her "bait." In her mouth is a rope tied to a stick holding up a box over the tacos. Ready for her unsuspecting prey, she calls out, "Here, lizard, lizard, lizard."

Unexpectedly, a threatening growl and imposing shadow steal the moment. A hungry and aggressive Godzilla appears. At the sight of the oversized monster reptile, the little dog promptly drops the rope and utters, "Uh-oh. I think I need a bigger box."

Like the little canine, we are all on a quest to find something that ultimately proves bigger than our expectation or capacity. Regardless, every soul searches. Some discoveries prove to be misguided. Others are completely transformational. Most are somewhere in between. In any case, we need the bigger and better box of a clear biblical understanding and a regular renewal in the truth of the one true God.

Have you ever considered that all of your life is ultimately an expression of your theology? Let's slow down here, as theology is not a topic usually discussed over breakfast or in casual conversation. The word comes from two Greek terms: *theos*, which means "God," and *logos*, which primarily refers to the "study of" something. For our purposes, we'll refer to it simply as "our view of God." This personal view exerts a great influence on us because everyone ultimately lives out his or her belief (or lack thereof) about the existence and character of God. This belief shapes our identity, forms our sense of purpose, and determines our real values in life.

Proverbs 9:10 and Psalm 111:10 tell us that "the fear of the LORD is the beginning of wisdom." Applying practical truth to daily life begins with our understanding of God. Knowing how we should live is anchored in the bedrock of our God-concept.

The first home my wife and I purchased was in the Seattle area. It was a new house. We were the first buyers in the neighborhood, so we selected our lot, floor plan, and preferences for the various amenities. Once construction began, we drove by our home-to-be virtually every day. It seemed like they took forever digging the trenches and pouring the solid foundation. Many weeks later, as we watched the walls, roof, exterior, and interior come together, we understood why the foundation was so essential. A carelessly done or incomplete foundation would have been the demise of the entire building. All the fine carpentry work, windows, doors, cabinetry, carpet, and paint would have ultimately been for nothing if the house crumbled on the moorings of a faulty foundation.

In life, we can be in such a hurry to create a strategic plan, build a career, and establish a family that we ignore the bedrock issue of a defined and applied theology. It is also a daily commitment. All of us can recognize and be renewed in this ground of solid truth. If we want a life that stands through the storms, it is essential. A. W. Tozer once noted, "The most important thing about a person is what comes to mind when they think about God."

What's on Your Plate?

I love all sorts of international foods. Chinese cuisine hovers near the top of my favorites list. Growing up, this was a simpler proposition. We would go into the restaurant, look at the menu, and order something that looked appetizing. We ate it and were happy—most of the time.

These days the Chinese buffet has grown in popularity. Recently, I was speaking in Florida, and my friend and host pastor Danny Hodges invited me to join him and his wife at a nearby restaurant. We strolled through multiple serving stations. Vast arrays of Chinese, Japanese, and American food presented countless choices. We could even create a Mongolian barbecue masterpiece with various combinations of meats, vegetables, and sauces. We also discovered multiple dessert stations. After a time of grazing and grabbing, the three of us returned to the table with plates full of food. Yet no plate was remotely similar to the others. We each utilized our options to design a unique masterpiece of culinary indulgence.

There was a day not long ago when theology was like ordering off a pre-set menu. The options were clear-cut. Today, our culture has taken advantage of the exploding list of options to create their own smorgasbord understanding of God. We've designed "gods" that work for us, based on our momentary appetites and attractions. Even the "nonreligious" box on personal surveys is being checked with unprecedented frequency, up to over 15 percent in 2010 from just 8 percent in 1990.[1] British preacher G. Campbell Morgan summarized our present moment well, even from his early-twentieth-century vantage point, by noting that when people lose their *consciousness* of God, they do not lose the sense of their *need* for God. They simply substitute the false for the true.[2]

When it comes to our view of God in today's society, almost anything goes. A plethora of Eastern religions are finding their way into the mix of modern-day "spirituality" with increasing influence. Allah is in the news every day in places where Islam was unheard of decades ago. Agnostics still aren't sure what they believe and are eager to invite you into the ranks of the undecided. Humanists continue to trust in their own shifting, man-centered ideas with resolute passion. Atheists are now featured on the bestseller lists of books and they have officially coalesced to poke fun at "less intelligent" religious people. A works-based approach to faith remains a culturally acceptable option for casual church attenders who hope good deeds will tip the eternal scales in their favor. Tozer warns, "Wrong ideas about God are not only the fountain from which the polluted waters of idolatry flow, they are themselves idolatrous. The idolater simply imagines things about God and acts as if they were true."[3]

Life, Breath, and All Things

The apostle Paul encountered a similar reality as he assessed and addressed the spiritually curious of his day: "Men of Athens, I perceive that in all things you are very religious; for as I was passing through and considering the objects of your worship, I even found an altar with this inscription: TO THE UNKNOWN GOD" (Acts 17:22–23). Not long ago, I stood in the very area called Mars Hill where Paul made these keen observations about the culture of his day. My visit to Greece reminded me that much has changed in that historic site. On the other hand, nothing has changed. The majesty of the acropolis and the beauty of the Parthenon have certainly lost their luster and influence since Paul stood in their shadow exchanging ideas with the philosophers of his day. Yet the cultural landscape of irreligious modern-day Greece still speaks of mankind's failed quest to discover a life-changing understanding of the one true God.[4]

Standing among the crowds, Paul went on to say:

> Therefore, the One whom you worship without knowing, Him I proclaim to you: "God, who made the world and everything in it, since He is Lord of heaven and earth, does not dwell in temples made with hands. Nor is He worshiped with men's hands, as though He needed anything, since He gives to all life, breath, and all things. And He has made from one blood every nation of men to dwell on all the face of the earth, and has determined their preappointed times and the boundaries of their dwellings, so that they should seek the Lord, in the hope that they might grope for Him and find Him, though He is not far from each one of us; for in Him we live and move and have our being, as also some of your own poets have said, 'For we are also His offspring.' Therefore, since we are the offspring of God, we ought not to think that the Divine Nature is like gold or silver or stone, something shaped by art and man's devising. Truly, these times of ignorance God overlooked, but now commands all men everywhere to repent, because He has appointed a day on which He will judge the world in righteousness by the Man whom He has ordained. He has given assurance of this to all by raising Him from the dead."
>
> Acts 17:23–31

In summary, Paul explains that all of man's attempts to find God through smorgasbord idolatry, man-made systems, and the religious trappings of buildings and icons reflect a wrong understanding of the one true God. We cannot erect a building high enough or a bridge far enough to reach God. Our efforts will crumble every time. In fact, He is the Creator, and He is working all around us to move us to find in Him real life and meaning. Now He is calling us to turn from our self-seeking and sin to His Son, Jesus Christ. This Christ has risen from the dead, proving His deity and validating the truth of His message. He is the one who will one day judge the world. Hear His call to your heart today.

The Solid Rock?

The compelling distinction of biblical Christianity is not that we must search for God by our own merits. Rather, He created us, loves us, is working in us to seek Him, and is ready by the merits of Jesus Christ to bring us into a true understanding of himself through a transforming relationship. A. W. Tozer says it this way, "God and man exist for each other and neither is satisfied without the other."[5] We learn this in Ephesians 2:1–10 (read carefully, even if this passage is familiar to you):

> And you He made alive, who were dead in trespasses and sins, in which you once walked according to the course of this world, according to the prince of the power of the air, the spirit who now works in the sons of disobedience, among whom also we all once conducted ourselves in the lusts of our flesh, fulfilling the desires of the flesh and of the mind, and were by nature children of wrath, just as the others.
>
> But God, who is rich in mercy, because of His great love with which He loved us, even when we were dead in trespasses, made us alive together with Christ (by grace you have been saved), and raised us up together, and made us sit together in the heavenly places in Christ Jesus, that in the ages to come He might show the exceeding riches of His grace in His kindness toward us in Christ Jesus. For by grace you have been saved through faith, and that not of yourselves; it is the gift of God, not of works, lest anyone should boast. For we are His workmanship, created in Christ Jesus for good works, which God prepared beforehand that we should walk in them.

It is beyond belief that the God of the universe desires to reconcile me to himself—that He found me, brought me to life, and drew me to His heart. God's rich mercy brought me life not because of my works of goodness but because of the good and gracious work of Jesus Christ. It is all the gift of God, and now He wants to work in me by His life to produce everything good in and through me.

The message of the Bible is unique, clear, and compelling in comparison to all the other religions of the world. It is still the life-transforming bestseller of all time, providing unchanging truth that continues to work for millions around the globe. Tim Stafford, in *Knowing the Face of God*, writes, "If the Bible carries one repeated message about God, it is that He wants to be known."[6]

Understanding this distinction provides a solid foundation for faith, identity, and meaning. Choose your foundation carefully. Your identity, purpose, values, priorities, goals, time, and ultimate legacy will all stand or fall on this foundation. The choice of self, doubt, or a smorgasbord creation of your own mind brings with it consequences, both temporal and eternal. When the true God is your choice, look forward to the adventure of an integrated life.

Prepare for Interference

So how do you implement a view of God in your life? Where does a person start? Perhaps the first important step is to recognize possible misconceptions and clear out the interference that blocks your view of God.

Years ago we had cable television activated at our house. The first few days we could not get clear reception on several of the channels. A few were nothing but snow, some barely discernible, some came in with minimal interference, while others were crystal clear.

I was finally motivated to call for repair when I couldn't watch *Monday Night Football*. After a house call, the serviceman informed us that a loose connection going into the TV set was causing the interference.

As I look back on that incident, it would have been foolish to be angry with the network because I couldn't get the game. The problem was *not* with the broadcast signal. It wasn't even a fault of the cable company's transmission capabilities. My connection was the one that was messed up.

It's like this in our view and understanding of God. He is sending all the signals necessary for us to get a clear picture of who He is. Sometimes we get angry with Him because the interference results in confusion, doubt, or frustration. Yet the problem is not with the sender. It's with our skewed reception. Confusing ideas about God can create considerable interference in our reception. Our view of God is affected by home environment, authority figures, and life experiences.

There is a sense in which our hearts and minds are like the camera on our smartphone with the record button always engaged. We come into the world spiritually receptive and hungry for truth. We record a lot of messages in the receiving center of our inner man. These files eventually are filled with all kinds of images and ideas—some good, some bad. It is important to assess what is on those files, where the messages came from, and the validity of their contents. Your theology needs to be based on the truth, not mere impressions from parents, teachers, classmates, enemies, failures, or crises—no matter how clear or distorted. Our erroneous views of God must be recognized, erased, and replaced with the truth that will set us free.

Recognizing God's Signal

The God who wants to have a living, intimate, daily relationship with us longs to be discovered by mankind, the object of His love. Increasingly, scientific discoveries point to a divine designer. In *The Case for a Creator*, Lee Strobel cites a conversation with the authors of *The Privileged Planet*, one an accomplished physicist/astronomer and the other a renowned philosopher. They state, "We've found that our location in the universe, in our galaxy, in our solar system as well as such things as the size and rotation of the Earth, the mass of the moon and sun and so forth—a whole range of facts—conspire together in an amazing way to make Earth a habitable planet. . . . And even beyond that, we've found that the very same conditions that allow for intelligent life on Earth also make it strangely well-suited for viewing and analyzing the universe. And we suspect this is not an accident. In fact, we raise the question of whether the universe has been literally designed for discovery."[7]

In the Bible, God reveals himself to call us to a compelling and accurate understanding of His character. He describes himself, for the sake of our understanding, in a variety of terms that help us to seek, know, and experience Him. (See appendix 1, "God's Self-Revelation.")

In His loving determination, God went even further than all of the biblical descriptions of truth in His written revelation. He so wants us to know Him that He entered our world to be seen, heard, and touched. His feet trod the streets of Jerusalem. Drops of His blood fell on the soil at Calvary. "In the beginning was the Word, and the Word was with God, and the Word was God." The gospel of John goes on to say, in chapter one (vv. 14–18), that we have seen His glory, "glory as of the only begotten of the Father . . . who is in the bosom of the Father, He has declared Him." Jesus is God's explanation of himself. So, if you want to have a firm foundation of truth upon which to base your life, study Jesus Christ.

Beyond creation, Scripture, and the incarnate Word, believers are empowered for spiritual intimacy by the indwelling truth of the Spirit of God. If I wanted my children to understand some truths in life, I would likely do three things: try to explain these truths, endeavor to demonstrate them, and even hire a personal tutor to assure that they are really learning these realities. God, in His perfection, has provided a personal indwelling tutor. The Holy Spirit is the very presence of God, illumining our minds and guiding our hearts to a transformational understanding and application of who He is.

This happens only as you commit yourself to the lordship of Jesus Christ as revealed in the written truth of God. Unless God indwells you, the basis for life decisions will forever be an insufficient support of facts and ideas. It will never be an integrated, firm foundation of truth.

God wants you to know Him even more than you want to know Him. When you make that commitment, by His resident power, knowledge, and wisdom, He will teach you about himself. As you spend time with Him and study about Him, you will grow in your love and understanding of Him. This is how to develop the firm foundation of truth for your life.

The "WIN" Begins

A. W. Tozer observes, "The greatest need of the human personality is to experience God himself. This is because of who God is and who and what man is."[8]

The second part of this book, "Discovery Exercises," is designed to help you take theological truth and daily experience God himself through your worship, integrity, and nonconformity. This process will help you begin to enjoy countless benefits as you open your mind and heart to the truth of God in precise ways to fuel renewal and reassurance.

The Theology Discovery Exercises will help you create and review regularly your own thoughts about our Lord Jesus Christ. Let me make two quick disclaimers. First, is the obvious fact that God cannot be reduced to words or human thoughts, let alone a written statement. This is only a place to begin. Second, writing your thoughts is a lifetime exercise that you'll edit and revise as you grow in the understanding of God's truth. Still, this is a starting point for highlighting and specifying the realities that touch your life at the deepest level.

Many of us might find ourselves living like practical atheists—our belief in God doesn't really change our lives. Nothing is dynamic until it is specific. That's why it's good practice to write down your view of God. As one man said, "Thoughts disentangle themselves when they pass through the lips and the fingertips."[9] Author William Faulkner said it this way, "I never know what I think about something until I've read what I've written on it."

Over the years I have been in the process of putting my answers to all eight questions in this book into written form. I have recorded these vital truths and listen to them regularly. Deuteronomy 6:4–9 says that certain revealed truths should be placed in front of our eyes, on our wrists, taught to our children, and written on our doorposts. Why? Because this information is to be worked into the fabric of our lives. I want to get up every morning knowing who God is, who I am in Him, knowing why I am here, what really matters, what I'm going to do, how I'm going to do it, and when it will be done. Ultimately, I want to finish well.

The most important life question is not about our career, where we live, how big our paycheck is, or even about our health. The most important question is "Who is God?" Yes, like Gidget the dog, we need a bigger and better box. Our Lord will provide it as we set our minds and hearts to know Him. The discoveries will spark a new beginning, a deeper journey, and new sense of spiritual victory—today and every day, for the rest of our lives.

If you are a brand-new Christian, it is good that you are making this discovery and commitment early in your spiritual journey. Perhaps you are still exploring the Christian faith. I trust you are even now sensing the grace of God calling to your heart to repent of your idolatry, trust Christ, and receive the gift of new life.

Maybe you have followed Christ for many years and realize today that you have neglected to live with a clear and vibrant daily renewal in the truth of who He is. Lay all regrets aside and with fresh Holy Spirit-birth resolve to begin again—today.

> 'Tis not enough to save our souls,
> To shun th' eternal fires;
> The thought of God will rouse the heart
> To more sublime desires. . . .
>
> How little of that road, my soul!
> How little hast thou gone!
> Take heart, and let the thought of God
> Allure thee further on.[10]

A Deeper Life Story

As each of us seeks to navigate the storms of life, we can discover the strength to survive and even thrive to the degree that we root our responses in unchanging truth. I have learned that I can focus on either what I feel, what I see with my limited perspective, or on what I know to be everlastingly true and transcendent.

Early in my pastoral journey I was called as the senior pastor of a church in deep turmoil. Their previous pastor of almost thirty years had been exposed after an extended extramarital affair. The church was embroiled in a 25-million-dollar lawsuit after being sued by a disgruntled member. They were in a financial tailspin. The people who remained felt betrayed and hurt. I soon learned that hurting people hurt others. At just thirty years of age, I became their leader. I had high hopes but soon realized the reality of being hurt and disillusioned.

A small group of "controllers" eventually sought to remove the elders, some of the staff, and their new young senior pastor (me) through a series of illegitimate accusations. The extended process of dealing with this group led to countless meetings, the recruitment of a mediation panel, and eventually a congregational vote of confidence. The church spoke overwhelmingly. The accusers lost and left the church. By then, my wife and I were ready to resign and find a different career path.

During those dark and confusing days, the journey looked very bad and felt even worse. Yet God gave me the grace to anchor my soul in the truth that He was consistently and completely good, even in the midst of chaos. The situation seemed out of control, but I was able to renew my mind in the transcendent truth that He was absolutely sovereign. The experience felt and looked very unfair as I absorbed much of the pain that existed even before my arrival at the church. Yet the truth that God is completely just in all His ways sustained my mind, will, and emotions.

I discovered that choosing to focus on the truth of God's character is the key to survival and sanity. This motivated me to clarify my working theology in order to experience this kind of powerful renewal every day and in any circumstance. I have learned that when my day begins with great thoughts of God, it powerfully affects my emotions and perspective throughout the day. The more I instinctively and specifically focus on the truth of His character, especially in difficult seasons of life, the more I experience a personal transformation and transcendence. The Holy Spirit uses truth to empower me to live with joy as I anchor my soul in the certainty of God's unchanging character. This has become the unshakable foundation for a deeper life and a daily win in the spiritual contest.

—Daniel Henderson

2

Who Am I?

I always wanted to be somebody. Now I realize
I should have been more specific.
                                        —Lily Tomlin

The glory of God is a human being fully alive.
                                        —Irenaeus

A healthy self-image is
seeing yourself as God sees you.
No more. No less.

The first public appearance in Jesus' formal ministry included a powerful pronouncement about His identity. As He came out of the water at His baptism, the Father declared from heaven, "This is My beloved Son, in whom I am well pleased" (Matthew 3:17). Immediately following this paramount moment, Jesus was led into the wilderness for a season of preparation through fasting and prayer. At the end of that time, Satan launched a direct attack, querying twice, "If you are the Son of God . . ." (4:1–11). At the core of Jesus' ministry was the truth of His heaven-affirmed uniqueness. At the heart of Satan's attack against Him was an attempt to question His true identity. The same tactics are used against every true follower of Christ.

Early Identity Crises

My first recollection of an identity crisis dates back to my childhood reading of *Are You My Mother?* In this story, a baby bird hatches while its mother is away and then wanders around his immediate world, asking, "Are you my mother?" He questions a dog, a swan, a heavy-machinery crane, a bulldozer, and anything else in his path. Each answer fails to provide the helpful information needed in his search for self-identity. Happily, at the conclusion of the tale, he does find his mother and the story ends well.

In some sense we all can understand this little bird's crisis. We have learned to ask in a more sophisticated manner, but we still wonder, *Am I significant? Where do I belong?* and *Who am I?* Counselor Larry Crabb says, "The basic personal need of each person is to regard himself as a worthwhile human being."[1] Sooner or later, we all face these foundational questions: What is the basis of my self-identity? How do I come to regard myself as worthwhile? Am I like the little bird, trying to discover my identity within my parentage or my immediate surroundings? Or can something, or Someone, more reliable help me discover who I am? Most important, will this discovery result in security—and integrity?

My friend Mark Batterson frames it well: "Most of us live our entire lives as strangers to ourselves. We know more about others than we know about ourselves. Our true identities get buried beneath the mistakes we've made, the insecurities we've acquired, and the lies we've believed. We're held captive by others' expectations. We're uncomfortable in our own skin. And we spend far too much emotional, relational, and spiritual energy trying to be who we're not."[2]

Based on our foundational beliefs about God, we instinctively form an understanding of our own essence. Regardless of our framework, I have found this premise to be true:

We all spend our lives either searching for, attempting to prove, or confidently expressing our identity.

The Basis of Your Identity

Some of us are still trying to figure out who we really are. Others have chosen a certain persona and are putting a great amount of time in establishing it before the watching world. We invest our energy in proving personal worth, acceptability, and value. Whether it is our images and postings on Facebook or the cleverness of our tweets, we are prone to project an image that is more about insecurity than our true identity.

Studies on the formation of identity have highlighted the growing confusion new generations face as they obsess on social media sites. One researcher concludes,

> Based on relevant existing research, it appears as though social networking sites negatively affect adolescent identity formation. They provide adolescents with the tools to divulge in self-centered behavior and trust virtual strangers. Adolescents are experiencing identity confusion at the time when they register for social networking profiles. They are vulnerable to meeting pseudo identities and having to distinguish between what is real and what is fake. The computer screen creates a distant mode of communication, in which the adolescent feels free to expose his or her desired identity without considering the consequences of his or her actions. Free online expression often results in skewed public perception and real-world management on the part of the adolescent, who is not emotionally equipped to handle it. Ultimately, adolescents must find a balance between their true and desired personalities.[3]

In our own way, we all try to prove ourselves, often using pretty strange attempts. Our fragile senses of significance may spring from our family name, personal achievements, physical appearance, or social connections.

Truly secure people are free from making "self" the point of reference in both thought and conversation. They become free of self-defeating comparisons, self-centered stories, and self-promoting actions. They are able to celebrate the worth and wins of other people with a genuine unselfishness. But, how to get there . . .

Wise Christians base their identity on the reliable foundation of biblical truth about God and what He says to be true. This becomes the key to a proper self-image. Our new and eternal life in Christ is the core of our true identity. Then, as we consistently renew our minds in His declarations of who we are, we can weather skewed input from the world, our unreliable emotions, and the trials of this life with confidence.

Through this process, I want you to know what Mark Batterson identifies as "the joy of discovering *who you are* and the freedom of discovering *who you're not*."[4] We are going to look at five different dimensions: eternal, experiential, external, essential, and effective. Each of these helps us to understand who we are. As a result, you will be encouraged to write out your essential and effective identity for the purpose of daily renewal using the Discovery Exercises in Part Two.

Our Eternal Identity

Man is a spiritual creature by God's design. In Genesis 1:27, the Bible specifically and distinctively describes this: "God created man in His own image, in the image of God He created him; male and female He created them." God breathed life's breath into man, and man became a living soul (2:7). From the beginning of time, we have been spiritual beings, distinctively formed apart from trees, animals, plants, or any other expression of God's creation.

Man is created with a spiritual capacity. Eternity is in our hearts. Deep within we are aware of realities beyond this physical life. We have a God-given yearning for something more.

Man's Unique Function in God's Plan

Spirituality is in vogue these days. Regardless of the varied expressions and strange stripes of all things "spiritual," it all points to the eternal core within. In unparalleled numbers our neighbors are searching for spiritual experiences through nature, meditative exercise, pop culture books, and religion.

Even after our ancestors rebelled, human beings continued to carry the unique image of God (Genesis 9:6). This verifies what some have termed the unequaled "soulical" dimension of man—his mind, will, and emotions. We've been given a unique ability for Godlike reason. And, unlike animals, human beings are endowed with the willful ability of moral choice. Mankind has a distinctive depth of spiritual emotion.

That doesn't stop the animated film industry, though, from trying to convince us otherwise. Whether it is Baloo the dancing bear, Eeyore the melancholy donkey, Nemo the adventurous fish, Remy the Parisian rat, or Simba the likable Lion King—it seems like animals are just like us. Even toys like Buzz and Woody and cars named Lightning McQueen and Sally Carrera teach us valuable lessons about life. Pretty soon we will believe that the animals and inanimate objects will someday write books, graduate from college, organize political parties, attend church, or celebrate birthdays. Maybe they'll build police stations, elementary schools, or monuments. They might even start having conferences on spirituality.

I think you get the point. God made mankind with this unique eternal cognizance, which is at the core of our distinction from the rest of creation. In all of this, He had a special design.

Spiritual on Purpose

As image bearers of God's life, we have been created for a purpose.

> Just as He chose us in Him before the foundation of the world, that we should be holy and blameless before Him. In love He predestined us to adoption as sons through Jesus Christ to Himself, according to the kind intention of His will, to the praise of the glory of His grace, which He freely bestowed on us in the Beloved.
>
> Ephesians 1:4–6 NASB

This potential allows us to interact meaningfully with God and with each other. Being able to relate beyond the physical will be with us for eternity, as each person is an eternal soul.

Early in my ministry I conducted some Christian apologetic lectures at the University of Virginia. During one visit, a graduate medical student invited me to tour the school's cadaver room. I went, not enthusiastically, for the experience.

What I saw in that massive room will never leave me. The pungent smell of formaldehyde filled my nostrils. Before me were scores of worktables occupied by the remains of people who had recently been active, living human beings. My gut knotted in response to the detailed inspection of the "specimens."

Later, during the long drive home, my mind filled with deep spiritual and emotional reflection. In those moments, physical existence seemed so very futile and fragile. Without eternal life (John 17:3) life's journey appears ultimately hopeless and without meaning. I thought about the people who live as if our brief journey on earth is nothing more than physical appearance and pleasure. They have nothing to look forward to but a six-foot hole, a crematorium, or a cadaver room. It is ultimate foolishness to ignore the spiritual dimension put within us by divine design.

Because we are spiritual beings, the real person will live beyond the grave. Every one of us faces an eternal destiny—a destiny determined by our theological foundation. It is either in heaven with our loving Creator or eternal separation from Him who granted us the ability to freely choose. Either way, we all face an eternal existence. This is our eternal identity, one uniquely true of all mankind.

A clear, biblical, and life-applicable answer to the question *Who am I?* breathes energy into all that follows. We can be "alive" with a clear sense of identity, purpose, and life direction when the reality of our relationship with God is a foundation for all of life's choices. Otherwise, life is just a cadaver.

Our Experiential Identity

You may remember the old movie *Short Circuit*, about a government-designed robot that escapes from its inventors. In seeking to interact with a vast new world of sight, sound, and people, it develops an independent intelligence and personality. In its quest for understanding, it constantly exclaims, "Input! Input! Number 5 needs input!"

That's how we live. As babies we yell, "Input! Input!" When we grow older, Mom or Dad may say, "A good child gets A's and B's, not C's and D's." Soon our value becomes rooted in performance or popularity. Our sense of worth becomes based on the unhealthy indicator of the opinions of others—even those who might befriend us on Facebook or follow us on Twitter.

Beethoven, in his early adult years, had a teacher who told him that as a composer he was hopeless. Thomas Edison's teacher told him that he was so stupid he would never learn anything. And when *Peanuts* creator Charles Schulz was in high school, the cartoons he drew for the school yearbook were unaccountably turned down. Input! Input!

Closer to our reality, we can all remember childhood nicknames. Most were not flattering. I remember being called "Dumbo" because my ears were apparently bigger than the average elementary school GQ model. Some lovingly referred to me as "Danny Fanny." While you are snickering, let me ask, "What did they call you on the playground?" Of course, we all responded "Sticks and stones may break my bones, but words. . . ." Yeah, right. We know this is all part of the flawed input of our journey.

From day one the environment in which we live and the people with whom we share it have been wielding strong influence on our self-perception. Unfortunately, the environment is spiritually toxic. The people who live in it are morally flawed because of sin. Their "input" is not a basis of our worth.

Ephesians 2:1–3 (NASB) describes well this toxic external environment and depraved internal world:

> You were dead in your trespasses and sins, in which you formerly walked according to the course of this world, according to the prince of the power of the air, of the spirit that is now working in the sons of disobedience. Among them we too all formerly lived in the lusts of our flesh, indulging the desires of the flesh and of the mind, and were by nature children of wrath, even as the rest.

Thanks to the choice of Adam and Eve, we are living as fallen creatures in a fallen system. As I heard someone once say, "Help! I'm being held prisoner by my heredity and environment." We can thank our God that the truth sets us free.

Satan's strategy continues to be the same for you and me as it was for our garden of Eden ancestors. He wants us to misunderstand God, to doubt His Word and character, then keep us in constant confusion in terms of who we are. Author and theology professor David Needham writes, "Sin . . . is the expression of an individual's response to the issue of meaning apart from the life of God."[5] Our sinful confusion about meaning and identity results in conflict, insecurity, and alienation in our relationships. And we will live defeated lives, just as our enemy has intended.

Our External Identity

When was the last time you stood in front of a mirror and took a good look at your truly unique image? You may have said, "I look really good in this new dress!" Or maybe you thought, *How did I get so old so fast?* Perhaps you secretly admitted, "I don't like myself." The problem is that your external reflection is not really you. It is only the packaging and a truly superficial indicator of your true worth.

It's pretty obvious that there's not much, outside of some intensive surgical procedures, that can be done to change physical appearance. But don't we try? Some are still trying to find value through making some body parts smaller, some bigger and others to look like another more "attractive" person. Somehow we have been fooled into thinking that image and identity is the same thing.

People with straight hair want curly, while those with curly hair want straight. Some without hair just want. Thin people desire more shape, heavy ones want less. Those who are light skinned seek to be darker, and some with darker tones want lighter. We are so confused! If only we understood that our good and sovereign God has uniquely formed each one of us, we wouldn't be so dissatisfied with our external identity.

The Bible says in Psalm 139 that before we were born, God determined our parts. He made us the way we are, and He doesn't make junk. There is divine design in the color of our hair, the features of our face, the size of our stature, and the type of our skin.

Limbs, Skin, and the Person Within

But what about someone whose image has been maimed since birth? If their identity is based on physical appearance or comparison with others, life is going to be tough. If the opinions of people about one's "attractiveness quotient" are vital to well-being, then trouble and heartbreak are inevitable. Certainly any tragedy that affects our physical appearance is unfortunate. But for those who have a strong foundation, it just affects the paint job. It doesn't cause the house to crumble.

At the time of this writing, I serve on the board of the National Association of Evangelicals. A fellow board member, Nick Vujicic, was born with tetra-amelia syndrome. This rare disorder caused Nick to be born without any of his four limbs. As he came through deep mental, emotional, and physical struggles in his early years, Nick eventually embraced his worth in view of the love, grace, and providence of God. Today he leads his own nonprofit organization, Life Without Limbs, giving motivational speeches worldwide about life with disabilities and the hope that can be found in the gospel of Jesus Christ. Nick is now married and celebrated the birth of their first child on Valentine's Day 2013. Nearly 70,000 people "liked" the photograph of their brand-new little boy named Kiyoshi James Vujicic that was posted to Facebook.

In a similar story of triumphant identity, I think of my friend Ken, one of the most inspiring people I've ever known. Back in the early 1980s, Ken was in dental school in the Chicago area. He and his fiancée were stopped at a light on an exit ramp next to a tanker truck filled with gasoline. Another large truck appeared in the rearview mirror. Suddenly, the approaching semi slammed into the back of the tanker. Ken and his fiancée were immediately engulfed in flames. She was killed. He had severe, life-threatening burns over most of his body. His very survival was touch and go for weeks. The pain and heartbreak were unbearable.

After months of excruciating treatments, multiple skin grafts, cosmetic surgeries, and ongoing therapy to help with his blood circulation, Ken started life over again. On the outside, he appeared completely different. But on the inside, Ken Campbell was still Ken Campbell—only stronger and better. Thanks to the power of God's Word and the enduring love of family and friends, he is more in touch with himself and His Lord than ever.

A national sports broadcast did a feature on Ken's life several years ago. Not only did Ken recover and become an avid runner, he competed in the Ironman Triathlon in Hawaii. Ken moved on to build a successful dental practice. He is a respected leader in local politics, an avid student of God's Word, and a model church member and ministry leader. Several years ago, Ken married a lovely Christian woman. He works hard on his rural ranch and has raised two beautiful daughters.

I love and respect Ken. Over the years I have learned that Ken is not his skin. Ken is the man who is within. Most people who know Ken don't even notice his extraordinarily scarred face and hands. We just know him as one of the finest individuals we've ever met.

Double—Even Triple Trouble

For many, this issue of our external identity is too intricately woven with our sense of real identity. A defect like Nick's or tragedy like Ken's would have been the doorway to unending despair. When we place too much importance on the "outside" without a solid understanding of the "inside," life is fragile and true integrity is doubtful. When this is added to the abundance of skewed data in our life's experience, we have double trouble.

Those who don't have Christ in their life have triple trouble. Their identity is based on the external and experiential—both of which are superficial and deceiving. Deep down inside, the eternal nature of their being struggles—not yet made spiritually alive. They aren't sure how to get a grip on these factors. The result can be a constant identity crisis. (See illustration below.)

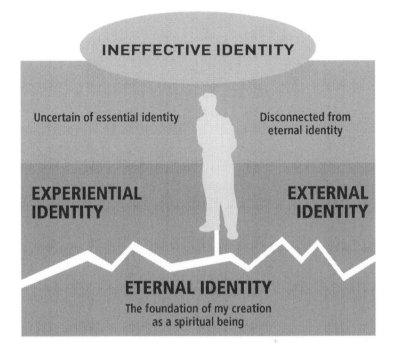

Our Essential Identity

So how does a person get past this emptiness and confusion? The answer is found in the dimension of essential identity. With spiritual birth comes a whole new reality in true identity. In fact, this new dimension supersedes all the others.

Essential identity reflects *Who am I?* in light of the person and work of Jesus Christ. This concept is best summarized in 2 Corinthians 5:17 (NASB): "If anyone is in Christ, he is a new creature; the old things passed away; behold, new things have come."

We are told that the power of Christ makes us new people. Colossians 3:3 (NASB) confirms this: "You have died and your life is hidden with Christ in God." Our pre-Christian identity is gone, dead by the power of Christ's death. Our new life and core identity is a reality because of Christ's resurrection and victory over sin and death.

We all typically use specific descriptors to identify ourselves to others. These may involve our race, place in the family order, height, specific appearance, and career. While these might be helpful, they are superficial. Our best self-description should be shaped by God's description of us. In the Discovery Exercises you will be guided to see yourself based on the absolutely true descriptions found in the Bible. When we learn to see and understand our identity from God's viewpoint, we can live by God's truth and empowerment.

In appendix 8 you will find a comprehensive list of the New Testament passages that give you God's truths about who you are in Christ. Make it a habit to read through this regularly as a powerful reminder of your new identity in Him.

Addition or Transformation?

When you came to Christ, your whole nature changed. You are not "just a sinner saved by grace." There's not an old nature and a new nature destined to dogfight for power and control. No, the Bible says you have been born again; you are a brand-new person, no longer a sinner as your essential identity, but a saint who happens to sin because of our vehicle of vulnerability—our flesh.

One author describes us as "spirit critters in an earth suit."[6] His point is that we're not sinners who received an addition of good things from God. No, it's not an addition. It is a transformation. We've gone from sinners to saints!

But you say, "I don't think of myself that way." That's the problem. We need to think of ourselves based on what God says. David Needham, author of *Birthright*, says, "A Christian is not simply a person who gets forgiveness, who gets to go to heaven, who gets the Holy Spirit, who gets a new nature. A Christian is a person who has become someone he was not before. A Christian, in terms of his deepest identity, is a saint, a born child of God, a divine masterpiece, a child of light, a citizen of heaven, not only positionally, not only judicially, but actually. Becoming a Christian is not just getting something, no matter how wonderful that something may be. It is becoming someone."[7]

Because you are in Christ, God sees you as He sees Him. Your old person died, was buried, and now you have risen as a new person. How can that be? It's because for God, there is no limitation of time. He chose you before the foundation of the world. When Christ died on the cross, you died; when He was buried, you were buried; when He arose, you arose. And now, with Him, you are seated in the heavenlies. This is spiritual reality.

A New Person on Assignment

But why are we left here in this earth suit to continue to struggle? Because the Lord has a mission for each one of us, an assignment to tell others about God's offer of this new life in Christ. This bleeds over to the next question: "Why am I here?" As we will see, purpose in life (or the lack thereof) springs from our sense of identity.

Years ago I spoke at a national conference in Phoenix. One illustration I used has helped many apply this reality. I spoke of how many believers tend to view their Christian faith as a cruise ship to heaven. We have our "ticket" (via a decision to follow Chist we made in church or elsewhere) and now are sailing to the celestial shore. The pastor is the cruise captain, whom we gladly beckon when things are not to our liking. The church staff is the ship's crew, and it is their job to be sure the menu of spiritual food and family services cater to our preferences. They also need to have the kind of music we like featured on the ship and stock the midnight buffet according to our tastes. A chocolate on our turned-down bed at night is also reasonable to expect.

With passion, I proclaimed that we are actually on a search-and-rescue battleship. We are only still sailing on earthly seas because we have an urgent mission to reach the lost at any cost. Jesus is our captain—and all of us are crew members serving under His command for the sake of others. That is a true understanding of how our new life is to find expression.

Our Effective Identity

I'll never forget the night I sat in a Seattle hotel enjoying a few moments of personal conversation with Bill Bright, founder of Campus Crusade for Christ. After a special event where we shared the platform, I asked his advice about some ministry struggles I was encountering. Among many other words of wisdom, he made this statement: "Every soul is precious, but not every Christian is strategic."

It is one thing to know how precious I am to God as a valued and loved child. It is another thing to be submitted to Him so that His power might turn my new person into a life of supernatural impact.

Our effective identity is all about who we are in the light of the design and enabling of God's grace. Great insight on this is found in Ephesians 2:10, where we read that we are His workmanship. You may remember that the Greek word here is *poiema*. Literally, we are His poem—His tapestry, His masterpiece. Each of us is specifically designed to make a difference in this world as an expression of our new life. As one writer says, "You are unlike anyone who has ever lived. But that uniqueness isn't a virtue. It's a responsibility. Uniqueness is God's gift to you, and uniqueness is your gift to God. You owe it to yourself to be yourself. But more important, you owe it to the One who designed you and destined you."[8] We are stewards of our unique, effective identity.

Discovering Your Spiritual DNA

To understand the factors of our unique usefulness I use the acronym S-DNA, which stands for our spiritual DNA. Just as we all have an exact physical code (DNA), so God has made every Christian unique in how they are wired for impact and service. The "S-DNA" represents spiritual gifts, desires of the heart, natural talents, and aptitudes. Seen as a whole, these form a distinct and effective identity.[9]

First, we need to understand and utilize our *spiritual gifts*. The Bible says, "Now there are varieties of gifts . . . to each one is given the manifestation of the Spirit for the common good" (1 Corinthians 12:4, 7 NASB).

God has given each believer unique gifts that enable us to minister with supernatural ability and impact for the glory of God. The fullness of effective identity is not possible until our spiritual giftedness is understood. In the Identity Discovery exercises in Part Two you will find an assessment for discovering your spiritual gifts.

We also have unique *desires of the heart* that express our God-given interests. "It is God who works in you both to *will* and to do for His good pleasure" (Philippians 2:13). God works through our desires to direct and motivate us in His purposes. For instance, God has shaped my heart to be passionate about preaching, catalyzing renewal through prayer, working with leaders, and connecting with strategic global missions efforts.

Other Christians might have desires to disciple children, reach young people, connect women to one another, promote social justice, or care for the poor in the local community. We each have a unique heart, and that's part of God's design for effectiveness in our identity for Him.

Through *natural talents*, we are empowered by God for effectiveness in His service. Exodus 36:1 illustrates this:

> Every skillful person in whom the Lord has put skill and understanding to know how to perform all the work in the construction of the sanctuary, shall perform in accordance with all that the LORD has commanded.
>
> NASB

We all have God-given abilities. Some people are good in science. God can use this. Others are good in music, and God brings forth effectiveness from this talent. Others are "prison singers"—always behind a few bars and never able to find the right key. Some have a talent to write. Many are good with mechanics, carpentry, art, sports, artistic design, or cooking. Our specific natural abilities are part of our effective identity.

Aptitude is an expression of our individual personality, work style, and approach to life. Over the years, through various assessments and experiences, I have learned that I am a conceptual thinker—an idea guy. I am an extrovert. My leadership style is inspirational and entrepreneurial. I am motivated to influence others. Knowing this helps me to recognize how and when God might want to use my unique design to His glory and others' good. This uniqueness within each person is a vehicle for God. As Paul wrote in 1 Corinthians 12:6, "There are varieties of effects, but the same God who works all things in all persons" (NASB).

Differences in aptitude can easily be seen in group dynamics. In an office, some workers are most productive in an organized environment where everything is in place. Others are comfortable with a little creative confusion. One person likes routine, another seeks variety. The same is true for families. Each household is made up of people with unique personalities. The best functioning families are those where parents respond to the differences in their children in a way that encourages development according to each individual aptitude.

When approaching a challenge, some of us work through it with our feelings first. Others think things through very logically and methodically. It's the same with extroverts and introverts, leaders and followers. We all approach life in a variety of ways, yet God brings effectiveness out of our differences.

Again, the Discovery Exercises will guide you to discover and then faithfully affirm and express your personal S-DNA for ultimate stewardship in serving others.

How to Experience Who You Are

Disney's version of the mysterious story of Anastasia, daughter of the deposed czar of Russia, reminds us that knowing our identity and living out that identity are not one and the same thing. She was a woman of royal birth and earthly notoriety. Yet throughout most of her life she had never known it. Neither did anyone else. She spent her adolescent years never understanding or experiencing her true identity. Known only as "Anya" in the orphanage where she grew up, Anastasia experienced a deep longing to know and be known by her family. Her passionate pursuit of this discovery propelled Anastasia on a journey that eventually led her to the home of her royal grandmother. Like every Disney movie, Anastasia's story ends happily as her quest for identity allows the princess to fully live the life for which she was destined.

Fullness of identity begins when you receive the message of the gospel of Jesus Christ as your only hope of salvation and a new life. The truth is that you carry the worth of God's Son. He cares so much for you that Jesus came and gave His life in order to provide you with a totally new one. By trusting His life and message, you can experience the gift of a new life.

Then, as Christ-followers living in the fullness of our new life, we must *recount truth about our new life and renew our mind daily*. Galatians 6:14–15 says, "May it never be that I would boast, except in the cross of our Lord Jesus Christ, through which the world has been crucified to me, and I to the world. For neither is circumcision anything, nor uncircumcision, but a new creation" (NASB).

Colossians 3:10 tells us that we are to "put on the new self who is being renewed to a true knowledge according to the image of the One who created him" (NASB). The key phrase is renewal to a "true knowledge." Paul reminded the Ephesian believers with a similar admonition: "Be renewed in the spirit of your mind, and put on the new self" (4:23–24 NASB).

To renew means "to make new again." Our integrity in life and nonconformity to the world depends on this commitment: "Do not be conformed to this world, but be transformed by the renewing of your mind, so that you may prove what the will of God is, that which is good and acceptable and perfect" (Romans 12:2 NASB). Transformation comes through renewing our mind according to God's truth. More important than putting on fresh clothes at the beginning of each day is the need to be renewed and clothed with our new identity in Christ.

Appendix 9 will give you an example of my essential identity statement and the unique mix of my S-DNA. Your goal, with help from the Discovery Exercises, will be to discover and clarify what is true about you. Once written, regular, meaningful review will empower you to be ready to default to these truths at any given moment of challenge or when facing thoughts of insecurity.

Soon you will be consistently living out your identity in Christ through regular and thoughtful review. Your essential identity will supersede the old experiential and external messages. You will be empowered to fulfill your eternal identity. This renewal will empower your effective identity in fulfilling His plan for your life.

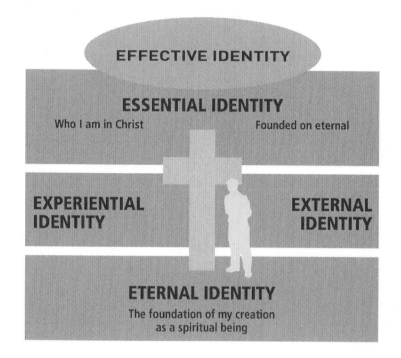

Soaring With the Eagles

The story is told about an eagle that was found by a farmer and raised among the barnyard ducks, chickens, and turkeys. It ate chicken food, drank out of the same container, and even behaved like a chicken.

One day, a naturalist visiting the farmer said, "That bird is an eagle, not a chicken."

"Well," replied the owner, "it may measure fifteen feet from wing tip to wing tip, but I raised it to be a chicken, so it no longer is an eagle."

"No," said the visitor, "it is still an eagle. It has the heart of an eagle and has been created to soar heavenward."

The farmer remained adamant. So they agreed to a test in which the visitor would have three days to make the majestic bird fly.

On the first day, even after much coaxing and encouragement, the eagle was more interested in jumping down onto the ground and joining the barnyard fowl for scattered grain. On day two, again being reminded that it had the destiny and heart of an eagle, the regal bird chose dirt, barnyard fowl, and chicken food.

On the third day, early in the morning, the naturalist took the eagle to a high mountain. Raising it up to survey the golden landscape and glistening peaks, the naturalist said, "You are an eagle. You belong high above, freely soaring through this expansive sky. Stretch your wings and fly."

The eagle looked over the valley below and hesitated. Taking the bird's head, the naturalist turned it directly toward the sun. An age-old quiver surged through the feathers and with a mighty shriek the bird flapped its powerful wings and soared toward the beckoning blue heavens.[10]

A deeper, thoughtful, intentional life flows from understanding who God is and then understanding who you are in Christ. A confident expression of one's identity is found in knowing—a secure knowing that is based on truth. This is the only sure foundation for a life of lasting integrity.

A Deeper Life Story

I worked hard to live with my priorities in order—God first; family second; and everything else third. However, work demands were great and the days were exhausting, leaving me with the longing to retire early so that I could have more time to focus on serving God and my family. I had developed a plan toward the goal of retiring at age fifty-five. After all, "failing to plan is planning to fail." So, like most successful businessmen, I mapped out a career path and navigated it effectively for nearly thirty years.

However, my path took a sudden detour when I turned fifty. My employment came to an abrupt end when an unexpected set of circumstances led to my resignation. By the time I had flown home from the corporate office—a ninety-minute flight—I had become "unplugged" from my successful career. I suddenly had no service on the work phone still in my pocket, no email, and no access to my office. Without an occupation or a title behind my name, I had lost part of my identity. After driving home from the airport that evening, I met with my friend Daniel Henderson over dinner. He helped me work through those first hours of unemployment as I began to process what God wanted to show me.

What I realized is that in the intense recent buildup of my five-year plan toward retirement, I had been missing a deeper encounter with God. Even though I stayed persistent in my daily reading of God's Word and remained actively involved in ministry, I still had a longing for a deeper relationship with my Savior.

As I write this, I am seven days into the "new plan." I recognized that the first steps of this plan were to discover who God is and who I am. I needed to transition from my experiential identity (what I did for a living) to my essential identity (who I am in Christ). I can now identify myself as **an authentic follower of Christ, created by an unconditionally loving God for the purpose of living my life in order to bring honor and glory to Him**. I look forward to discovering my essential identity, my spiritual DNA, so that I can utilize the gifts He has given me in a way that allows others to see Christ reflected in me.

I'm realizing that God's new plan is moving me from success in my career to significance in His kingdom. By renewing my mind daily in a deeper understanding of my true identity, I know that I can trust God as He leads me **today**. There is no need to worry about tomorrow or the plan that will unfold in five years. There is a purpose for me today that God wants me to discover. When I do return to the work force, it will not be business as usual. As my future begins to unfold, I am determined not to run ahead of God as I follow His plan—one step at a time.

—A. E. Brown

3

Why Am I Here?

The great tragedy in life is not death but life
without reason.

— *Myles Monroe*

David, after he had served the purpose of God
in his own generation, fell asleep, and was laid
among his fathers.

— *Acts 13:36*

Many of us spend our lives chasing after things that the world
convinces us we must have in order to be significant. Competition for the most innovative technology dominates the marketplace
and feeds our desire to distinguish ourselves in the race to get ahead.
An AT&T TV commercial even implies that surfing and talking
at the same time will provide the satisfaction we seek by asking,
"What's better, doing two things at once or just one?"

Sadly, the generation most proficient at using technology to help
multitask also seems to be the least satisfied. In a recent national
survey, Millennials (adults ages eighteen to thirty-four) reported
the highest stress levels of any generation.[1] In our quest for satisfaction, we'll eagerly pursue the latest phone to hit the market yet
continually delay searching for the truth of who God is, who we
are, or why we're here.

Let's stop multitasking for a moment and reflect on something of primary importance: why Jesus came. He alone can provide the satisfaction you seek. He can set you free from the drumbeat of this world, free from the influence and expectations of other people. He can provide freedom from your burden of stress as you get to know Him and know who you are in Him. Whether or not your phone surfs while you talk is secondary.

Interrupted Purpose

I remember the time I was having dinner at a friend's house and inadvertently dropped my cell phone in the toilet (evidence of my own obsession with multitasking). In fact, phone repair centers tell you this is the most common reason phones are ruined. If you've ever lost functionality on your cell phone, with no ability to connect to the people and information important to you, you've felt the frustration of a device that no longer serves its intended purpose.

In the movie *Hugo*, an orphaned boy is desperate to repair a broken machine called an automaton. Convinced that this mechanical man holds a secret message from his father, Hugo struggles to make the necessary repairs in the hope of finding a purpose for his life. Disappointed by his inability to fix the contraption, the twelve-year-old observes, "Maybe that's why a broken machine always makes me a little sad, because it isn't able to do what it was meant to do. . . . Maybe it's the same with people. If you lost your purpose, it's like you're broken."[2]

It's apparent in our world today that many people are broken. They have no idea why they are here. Until we understand our purpose, life really has no meaning. The fact is, God wants you to live a life of significance, a life that is clearly yours because of Him. Young Hugo later explains his philosophy regarding a purposeful life to his childhood companion Isabelle: "Machines never come with any extra parts, you know. They always come with the exact amount they need. So I figured if the entire world was one big machine, I couldn't be an extra part. I had to be here for some reason. And that means you have to be here for some reason, too."[3]

We are all on this earth for a reason. The Amplified Bible describes this as "a divinely implanted sense of a purpose working through the ages which nothing under the sun but God alone can satisfy" (Ecclesiastes 3:11). Proverbs 16:4 explains, "The LORD has made everything for its purpose, even the wicked for the day of trouble" (ESV). Surprisingly, the Bible says God has a purpose for people who do not obey him: "For the Scripture says to the Pharaoh, 'For this very purpose I have raised you up, that I may show My power in you, and that My name may be declared in all the earth'" (Romans 9:17). Trying to get your head around that idea may be challenging. However, getting your head around the fact that He has a purpose to use you in this life for His glory is the great need of the moment.

God offers you an opportunity to live a life that, when it is over, you can look back and know that you lived well. I've heard it said many times, "You're not really ready to live until you know what you want written on your tombstone." If you were to die today, would those who know you be able to say, "This is why _____ lived"? Is it clear to you why you are here? When this life comes to an end, will you look back and conclude that you have lived well and significantly?

Most of you have probably seen some version of Scrooge in *A Christmas Carol*. Perhaps the most significant event in this memorable story is the transformation of Mr. Scrooge's perspective on life. After investing his days in greed and self-centered living, he receives a vision of how his life might end. He is kneeling before a neglected grave, and after reading the gravestone that bears his name, he is jolted by the realization that there are far more important things in life than the petty focus that has always consumed him. From that moment on, Ebenezer Scrooge devotes his energies toward a new mission in life. What changed him? He realized that he was living for the wrong reason. When he came to terms with the possible outcome of his lifelong course, his whole purpose for living changed. So can yours.

A meaningful life requires purpose. This is true of groups, societies, churches, families, relationships, and individuals. "History shows," voiced one observer, "that the value of life decreases and the quality of existence diminishes when a generation loses its sense of destiny and purpose."[4]

Advantages of a Well-Defined Purpose

Answering the question *Why am I here?* provides a sense of clarity in a way that will set you on a course that will ultimately give your life definition and enduring significance. Let's explore some of the advantages that a well-defined purpose will add to your life.

Meaningful Destination

As we have said, some people spend their life climbing the ladder of success and find it has been leaning against the wrong wall. To realize that all of one's efforts were for nothing, that it was all meaningless vanity, is a sorry way to finish.

But when we come to Christ and understand who He is and who we are, we acquire a sense of purpose. We have a destination that matters. The journey proves to be valid.

In 1 Corinthians 9, Paul uses the analogy of athletes who give their all but end up with a prize that is perishable. In our day it would be like an Olympic runner who sacrifices his or her life in order to run a race that results in a medal (that could get lost) and the possibility of being pictured on a cereal box (that will likely be thrown away). Paul says that while many run for a perishable prize, Christians run for a prize that is imperishable. We have a destination that is forever. People who come to terms with Christ's plan and purpose for them have a destination that is meaningful.

Clear Direction

Another benefit of purpose is that it provides your journey with clear direction. You have knowledge of the way you should go in order to get to where you're supposed to be. As Paul says, "I run in such a way, as not without aim; I box in such a way, as not beating the air" (1 Corinthians 9:26 NASB). Just any road won't do for him. Paul knows his purpose and his direction.

Our GPS tools, available in a variety of formats, are only as good as our clarity about the destination we are seeking. Without a specific address, the device only tells us where we are, not where we need to go. Purpose is the destination of the earthly journey. When it's clear, we know when to turn, when to go straight, when to make a U-turn, and when to recalculate.

Today's society is confused and without direction. Students enter college looking for direction but quickly get discouraged and frustrated. There are now vast numbers of universities where the four-year graduation rate is less than 30 percent.[5] Young people are entering the job market not knowing what career to choose or which path to follow. Adults, too, lack focus. The solution ultimately has to do with the question of purpose. When you know that, you know your direction.

Powerful Determination

Purpose also instills within us the power of determination. Years ago I heard insurance executive Charles "Tremendous" Jones say, "You can tell someone what to do and they may do it for a little while. But once they believe in why they are doing it, it will take a brick wall to stop them." Even philosopher Friedrich Nietzsche, who denied his faith early in life and became a critic of Christianity, shows he understood the value of purpose when he stated, "He who has a *why* to live can bear almost any *how*."

So many people just give up. We live discouraged lives because we forget why we're here. Comedian Louis Grizzard noted, "Life is like a dogsled team. If you ain't the lead dog, the scenery never changes." Without a sense of purpose, we feel like we are just buried somewhere in the pack with no clear understanding of where we're headed.

Conversely, when we understand the meaning behind it all, we run with clarity, direction, and passion. Truly strong and enduring lives are motivated by dynamic purposes.

Even though the noise of life screams for our attention and the troubles of life attempt to derail us, knowing the "why" behind it all keeps circumstances in perspective. Purpose gives us real assurance that "all things work together for good to those who love God, to those who are called according to His purpose" (Romans 8:28).

After her diagnosis of breast cancer in 1998, Stefanie Spielman, wife of former NFL star Chris Spielman, began to embrace her purpose in life. During her eleven-year battle with the disease, she and Chris raised several million dollars for breast cancer research. But Stefanie's purpose went much deeper than raising funds for this important cause. Stefanie's daughter Madison recently reflected, "She never once questioned God's plan for her, and instead of sitting around feeling sorry for herself, she stood up and did something about it. When asked why she thought she had to go through all the pain and suffering cancer brings, she simply smiled and said, 'Why not me?'"[6] Though she was only fifteen when her mother died, she was clearly impacted by the joy her mother brought to others. "She gave hope to those who thought it no longer existed," writes Maddie. "Soon after my mom passed away, we received a letter from a woman my mom had spoken to several years earlier. In her letter, this woman told how she had spoken to my mom to thank her for everything she had done to fight cancer and give people hope. My mom looked at her in surprise and, after a moment's hesitation, said, 'Don't you understand? That's why I'm here.' My mom knew her purpose on this earth, and she welcomed the challenge with open arms."[7]

Internal Delight

Last, but not least, purpose infuses your experience with a sense of delight. That doesn't make the journey easy, just worth it. Helen Keller said, "Many persons have the wrong idea of what constitutes true happiness. It is not obtained through self-gratification, but through fidelity to a worthy purpose." A worthy purpose brings joy.

Jesus knew that. In Hebrews 12 we are told to fix our eyes on Jesus, "the author and perfecter of faith, who for the joy set before Him endured the cross . . ." (v. 2 NASB). Is it possible to endure, with joy, the crosses in life? If your answer is no, then the issue may be one of purpose.

This is why the early church counted unpleasant circumstances a joy and privilege, even in persecution. They had a reason for existing, and it was not grounded in personal popularity and acceptance. They were driven by a mission—the mission of Jesus in their lives. If that is true in your life, it will infuse you with delight no matter the situation.

Multipurpose Purposes

Three aspects of purpose are important as we seek to renew our minds in truth and live a deeper existence. They are eternal, earthly, and explicit. *Eternal purpose* is the overarching reason for our existence, not just in this life but for eternity. Our *earthly purpose*, which we will use interchangeably with the idea of mission, helps us to identify why we are here on earth—right here, right now. Even more specific expressions we will call *explicit purposes*. These bring meaning to the varying roles in our lives. The Purpose Discovery exercises, found in Part Two, will help you clarify your own eternal, earthly, and explicit purposes; but first, here's an overview.

Eternal Purpose

A clear understanding of eternal purpose is rooted in theology and identity. When you remember that God is the Creator, your existence has divine intention. When you know yourself as an eternal soul redeemed for eternity, you know that you exist for realities beyond this temporary life.

So why do you exist? Isaiah 43:6–7 says, "Bring My sons from afar, and My daughters from the ends of the earth—everyone who is called by My name, whom I have created for My glory; I have formed him, yes, I have made him." Romans 11:36 repeats this truth: "For of Him and through Him and to Him are all things, to whom be glory forever. Amen." Here, as in other biblical texts, we are reminded that we are created by Him and for Him.

These truths likely motivated the Westminster Catechism, which concludes: "The chief end of man is to glorify God and to enjoy

Him forever." This is the real purpose for our existence. That's why we are here and why we will live forever.

At a personal level, I have thought about a statement that reflects my understanding of God's eternal purpose for my life. Although it is almost impossible to improve upon the Westminster classic, I have rewritten my own version in this way:

> *I exist to worship, glorify, and enjoy God forever in an authentic love relationship with Him through His Son and my Savior, Jesus Christ.*

Earthly Purpose

Our earthly purpose is our mission here on earth. This is the "why" behind our brief journey on this earth. Can you specifically and passionately articulate your mission on earth? You have one, you know. You do not need to "develop" it. God already has made you to fulfill it. All you need to do is discover it, live it deeply, and complete it. As one person put it, "Here's the test to find whether your mission on earth is finished: If you're alive, it isn't."[8]

The New Testament's many teachings about how to live fruitfully as a Christian encourage us to remember that we were created by, through, and for Jesus Christ (Colossians 1:16; Hebrews 2:10). As we've already seen, our effective identity fits us perfectly to fulfill our mission, "For we are His workmanship, created in Christ Jesus for good works, which God prepared beforehand that we should walk in them" (Ephesians 2:10).

When the Lord saved you and made you His, He could have called you immediately into His presence. Your worship would have become much fuller, your knowledge more complete, and your fellowship with Him perfected. He has left you here on a mission. Remember? *Search and rescue.* This is true of every believer who has been reconciled to God through Jesus Christ.

Much has been written about personal mission statements, as seen from a business or corporate point of view. Even so, you'll discover great benefit in writing a personal statement, then praying over it and making it a vital part of your daily experience. Of course, your purpose will be based on your foundational theology and identity, thus rooted deeply in God's truth and not merely some personal whim or ambition for accomplishment.

An earthly purpose, or mission statement, should remain fairly constant, regardless of age, roles, relationships, setting, location, status, or health. It represents a guidepost for everyday living. Here is my earthly purpose or mission statement:

My mission is to fully experience and faithfully express the life of Jesus Christ leading to fresh encounters of His person and presence among the saved and the lost.

Certainly this may not be necessary for you, but I have a little formula that helps me remember my mission: FE (Fully Experience) + FE (Faithfully Express) = FE (Fresh Encounters). For me, the idea of "fresh encounters" is rooted in the title of a book I previously wrote and the description we gave to our weekly prayer meetings at our church for many years. So it is a term that has personal meaning. The Word and Spirit of God will help you craft one that will be memorable and meaningful to you.

Explicit Purposes

Explicit purposes become a more specific application of your mission. This happens when we clarify the purpose of our daily roles and relationships. For instance, you can discover and write your specific purpose in your roles as a parent, an employee, a volunteer at church, etc. Although it is possible to get carried away and end up with so many statements that you lose the substance, the Purpose Discovery exercises (Part Two) will guide you step by step.

Like your earthly purpose, defining your explicit purposes starts with *why*—why you work a certain job or why you parent, for example. A good working definition of *purpose* for this exercise is "the subject in hand" or "the point at issue."[9] So if you are a mother, your current "subject in hand" is your child. One example of an explicit purpose statement for this role might be:

My purpose as a mother is to seek God's guidance and raise my children with no regrets, putting their interests above my own.

The "roles and relationships" purpose statements obviously will vary because these elements of our lives can change over time. Yet your earthly purpose will remain fairly intact, while your eternal purpose is a constant.

Discovering Your Purpose

The goal of this daily renewal process is to experience clarity and conviction, leading to a compelling sense of purpose. So as you work through the application exercises, consider the following:

The Starting Point: Relationship

Your purpose should reflect the will of God for your life. To best understand a person's desires or intentions, we must have a familiar relationship with that individual. You could ask me about the will of Kate Middleton on some matter and I would not have a clue because I do not have a relationship with her and never will. Ask me what my wife desires or wills on some issue, and I would likely have a solid answer.

If you want to know the heart and mind of your Creator concerning His purpose for your life, you need a relationship with Him. He offers this through the work of His Son, Jesus Christ. Recognizing the unique claims and deity of Christ and trusting Him as the One who can save you from your sins and rule your life is the first step toward purpose. You can become the new person we spoke of in the previous chapter and effectively be in a relationship that will provide the lifeline for your purpose discovery.

Purposeful Truth

God's will is revealed in God's Word. Faithful study and growing familiarity of the Scriptures, especially the Gospels and New

Testament guidelines for daily living, will guide you to discover biblical and eternally significant purposes.

Trusting His Sufficient Guidance

We're not left to our own energy or reason in discovering truth to shape our purpose. As Christians, we are inhabited by the Holy Spirit. As you seek to articulate clear purposes for your life, rest in this assurance:

> As it is written: "Eye has not seen, nor ear heard, nor have entered into the heart of man the things which God has prepared for those who love Him." But God has revealed them to us through His Spirit. For the Spirit searches all things, yes, the deep things of God. For what man knows the things of a man except the spirit of the man which is in him? Even so no one knows the things of God except the Spirit of God. Now we have received, not the spirit of the world, but the Spirit who is from God, that we might know the things that have been freely given to us by God.
>
> 1 Corinthians 2:9–12

Living in His Steps

The Bible consistently reaffirms that Jesus came with a clear sense of mission. All of the works, miracles, and deeds of Jesus ultimately flowed from His mission of being born to die in order that we might live. His mission was to shed His blood on the cross so that you and I might receive the forgiveness of sins and that He might give eternal life through himself. He came to give you a reason for existing here on earth, and He wants you to know why you are here.

Appendix 6, "Titles and Names of Jesus," includes many verses in which Jesus Christ reiterates His purpose, noted with phrases such as:

"I came [for this purpose . . .]"

"The Son of Man has come that . . . "

"I have come that . . ."

The Bible consistently reaffirms that Jesus came with a clear sense of purpose. One of these declarations occurred early in the ministry of the Lord when He visited the town of Capernaum. After amazing everyone with His teaching, He then demonstrated His power by casting out demons and healing various sicknesses. Naturally, the people of the town wanted Jesus to remain with them, but He responded that He must proclaim the good news of the kingdom of God to the other towns also, because that is why He was sent. Jesus stayed focused on His purpose in order to fulfill His mission on earth.

Following in Christ's steps brings new meaning to the hours you're investing in that job, hobby, or volunteer commitment. A wise man once said, "Great minds have purposes. Others have wishes." Are you spending your life wishing and wondering, or do you have a God-given purpose that compels you? Until this is clear, you will be confused about what you should be doing with your time, resources, and direction.

Clear and Compelling

It may take time, but eventually you will find the right words that capture the vital essence of your eternal, earthly, and explicit purposes. Again, by writing, praying, rewriting, studying, getting feedback, and writing again, it will become clear.

Instant Recall

As I and countless others have discovered through this process, there is great power in instant recall. When your days feel meaningless, your emotions are wacky, your direction is fogged, and your ears and head are filled with the disturbing dictates of the world around you, your purposes can prevail. Think about them, pray about them, speak about them, and live in light of them every day.

So, What Will You Do?

I've heard and told the story of the three bricklayers many times. You've probably heard it too, but the relevance is obvious as we wrap up this chapter.

Once there were three bricklayers working together. A passerby asked each one what he was doing. The first man answered gruffly, "I'm laying bricks." The second man replied, "I'm putting up a wall." The third man said enthusiastically, "I'm building a great cathedral where people can encounter God, families can find refuge, and society can be served."

A deeper life embraces the noble purposes of God for everyday life. We are not just fulfilling mundane tasks. We are not simply working on temporary projects. We are joining the God of the universe in a plan that matters for eternity. "Why am I here?" is an essential question for strategic daily renewal and the experience of winning over the devil, the flesh, and the world around us. God has a place for everyone, and everyone can find their place. Now go build that cathedral.

A Deeper Life Story

Daniel Henderson was gracious (and brave) enough to be a guest speaker at our moms' group. After Daniel shared his eloquent personal mission statement, we were all inspired to consider our eternal, earthly, and explicit purposes. I began thinking on the way home that night (as my boys were fighting) about a simple statement that described my purpose. It needed to be brief because my attention span is short. "Make an impact" immediately came to mind. After getting home and turning on the television, I noticed the title of a movie—**The World Is Not Enough**. It struck me that adding it to my statement would work beautifully—"I want to make an impact because this world is not enough."

Oh how thankful I am that this world is not the end and that no matter how old we are or what position we hold in life, we can still have an impact. I was twenty-four weeks pregnant when I was told that my child would be born with severe congenital heart defects. The pediatric cardiologist was not sure how long the baby would live after he was born. The team of fourteen doctors attending the birth anticipated the delivery of a small baby. When Ian David made his appearance on Mother's Day 1998, he weighed in at 9 lbs. 3 oz. It was apparent Ian was born with a purpose in life. After undergoing two heart surgeries over the next nine days, our miracle baby came home with us in time to celebrate Memorial Day. But the miracles didn't stop there. At nine months of age, Ian underwent a major surgery that left him on the heart/lung bypass machine for five days. He shouldn't have lived, but he came home three weeks later. He walked, he talked, and he went to school. He rode a bike, and learned to swim. He was also the best big brother possible.

Ian endured five more heart surgeries, numerous bouts with pneumonia, and complications beyond comprehension. But it didn't thwart God's purpose for Ian's life. God gave Ian a special group of people to impact in a way that I never could. Ian simply radiated God's love through his kindness and attitude. It was noticed by his doctors and nurses, as well as his classmates and their parents.

God took Ian to heaven shortly after he turned seven.

Over the years since Ian's homegoing, we keep hearing how much he touched people's lives. I could never have had that strong of an impact on all of those people. My mission is to make an impact on my children. It was then furthered by my son. Isn't that what everyone wants—to impact a person who in turn impacts others?

—Amy Mapes

4

What Really Matters?

Ideas go booming through the world louder than cannons. Thoughts are mightier than armies. Principles have achieved more victories than horsemen or chariots.

—W. M. Paxton

Back of every noble life there are principles that have fashioned it.

—George Lorimer

And also if anyone competes as an athlete, he does not win the prize unless he competes according to the rules.

—The Apostle Paul

Growing up, one of my favorite games was Monopoly. I have fond memories of Friday nights at my older brother's home, fiercely competing to put one another out of business through our dominant real estate holdings. I am not sure that I ever actually read the official rules for Monopoly. I just adapted to the rules my brother taught me.

As I've played Monopoly over the years with other friends and acquaintances, I've realized that many of us have made up our own rules about how and when to collect money, when you can and cannot start trading properties, and how you can manipulate things when you are about to go bust. When people play the same game using different rules, conflict and confusion ensue.

In life, many of us are playing by rules we learned somewhere and from someone along the way. We value our rules, which may or may not be based on reliable truth. We soon realize that other people have their own sets of rules. Not only can we become confused on how the game of life is to be played, conflict abounds as our values clash with those of others. Of course, Monopoly is just a game of little consequence. Life, on the other hand, is a contest that requires clarity and conviction about the principles that make for satisfaction and significance.

A Crisis in Values

Researcher George Barna has alerted us many times to the waning framework of American values. In one study, he discovered, by a three-to-one margin, adults said truth is relative to the person and their situation. Among teenagers, 83 percent said moral truth depends on the circumstances, and only 6 percent believed moral truth is absolute. More disturbing was Barna's discovery that only 32 percent of "born-again" adults said they believed in moral absolutes, while only 9 percent of born-again teens believed truth was uncompromising.[1]

In today's culture, it is officially old school to live by values rooted in absolute truth. At a young age, most Americans are exposed to the worldview of relativism and the importance of tolerance. The new "truth" of our society is the what-works-for-you philosophy apart from any foundation of unchanging reality.

President Ronald Reagan weighed in many years ago when he said, "We don't expect children to discover principles of calculus on their own, but some would give them no guidance when it comes to ethics, morality, and values."[2] Another former president lamented the values of today: "If it feels good, do it, and if you've got a problem, blame somebody else."[3] Speaking of presidents, I remember a cartoon depicting the young George Washington. He had just cut down the cherry tree and was saying to his father something like, "My teacher says I cannot tell a lie, I cannot tell the truth, and I cannot tell the difference."

Give Us This Day Our Daily Relativism

Today, we live in an age of pervasive relativism. It's found in business, education, and politics. We also experience it in family life and even in religion. Closer to the home of our own hearts, many of us live our everyday lives in a relativistic fashion. We embrace the idea of values but have not clarified what they are and how they should scaffold our daily lives. When it comes to values and issues of principle, we have our feet firmly planted in midair. It's hard to go deep or win the daily battle with that approach to life.

As I mentioned before, a few years ago I was called as the senior pastor of a church in deep trouble. After substantial campus relocation, the congregation was strapped with an eighteen-million-dollar mortgage, a ten-million-dollar cash shortfall from a failed capital campaign, and no senior pastor. The preacher confessed to adultery just six weeks after the relocation.

In the process of seeking to shepherd the church to health and guide the staff, I conducted an experiment a few months after my arrival. For years, the church had emphasized fifteen guiding principles that uniquely identified their congregation and clarified their ministry strategy. So, at an all-staff gathering, I handed out blank sheets of paper and asked the staff to list these fifteen values. I was met with blank stares. After collecting the papers, I discovered that one staff member listed five, most could recall one or two, and some had no idea what I was talking about. It mattered little if the church had five or fifteen key values. What did matter is whether the leaders understood and "owned" them as essential and relevant to the ministry.

Many of us function this same way in our daily experience. We know truth is important. Somewhere, someone wrote about   79 it—we seem to recall. We feel the need to clarify the things that really matter. But we lack any definition, compelling recall, or clear articulation of the "rules of the game" in our lives.

Our Set of Working Values

What if someone were to come up and ask, "Can you explain your values in two minutes or less?" Could you identify some uncompromising principles that are real for you and woven into the fabric of your daily existence? Are they so clear and dominant in your thinking that they are a framework for your daily life? Do you have a certain awareness that these principles spring from the Word of God?

I believe every one of us has a longing to embrace wisdom in such a specific way that it results in a system of principles that will guide and guard our daily journey. We need a set of personal convictions that we will not compromise. This can be described as a value system.

Paul reminds us in 2 Timothy 2:5, "If anyone competes as an athlete, he does not win the prize unless he competes according to the rules" (NASB). As we affirmed in the early pages of this book, we want to win the daily contest through a life of worship, integrity, and nonconformity. Values matter. A clear understanding of the unchanging rules of the game matters.

Declared vs. Demonstrated

When it comes to values, I see two important factors. One is what I call our declared values; the other involves our demonstrated values. Declared values are what we say. Demonstrated values give evidence to what really matters by how we live. To avoid the dilemma of double-minded living and practical hypocrisy, we must come to a point where these two factors align.

It reminds me of a story someone told me years ago about a young, devout, unmarried seminarian. Newly graduated, he knew what he believed, and he valued sincerity, truth, and honesty. That is, until one day when he boarded a plane. Sitting there, he noticed a beautiful young lady coming down the aisle. He found it hard not to stare as she attracted his rapt attention. Sure enough, she sat down right beside him. Then she opened her Bible and started to read. *There is a God in heaven,* he said to himself, *and He is smiling upon me!*

He started a conversation with her, having first checked to make sure she had no wedding ring. After some casual talk, he decided to be more direct. "What kind of men do you like?"

"That's an interesting question," she replied. "This may be unexpected, but I like Native American men. They really have a sense of heritage and history. They know who they are, and they're powerful.

"But," she continued, "I've known some Jewish fellows also, and what a sense of morality and heritage and principle they have. I really enjoy their friendship. Still, to be very honest with you, my favorite kind of guy is just a country boy. They're so honest and down-to-earth and easy to know."

The seminarian was deep in thought when she decided to ask him a question. "By the way, what is your name?" The young man, with temporary value amnesia, moved closer to her and replied, "Oh, my name is Geronimo Goldstein, but my friends just call me 'Bubba.'"

What's in Your Equation?

If we thought about it, most of us live somewhere *between* our declared and demonstrated values. Jesus often addressed the religious leaders and fickle followers of his day about the contradiction between what they "believed" and how they lived.

For example, in Luke 6:46 Jesus says, "Why do you call Me 'Lord, Lord,' and not do the things which I say?" And Paul's letter to Titus speaks of those who profess one thing but do another: "They profess to know God, but in works they deny Him" (1:16).

The task before us, if we are to live an integrated, meaningful life, is to come to a place of clarity and regular application so that our *declared* and *demonstrated* values are consistent and complimentary, not contradictory. A shallow, occasional engagement with the vital issue of values will not create a satisfying life. We must go deeper.

This idea can be stated as an equation:

$$Declared + Demonstrated = Integrity$$
$$Declared - Demonstrated = Hypocrisy$$

V. Gilbert Beers, former senior editor of *Christianity Today*, said, "A person of integrity is one who has an established system of principles against which all of his life is judged."

In the previous chapter, we described how Stefanie Spielman discovered her purpose in the wake of her breast cancer diagnosis. For the Spielmans, the life-shattering news came in the summer of 1998, just as Chris was preparing for his tenth season in the NFL. Having often quoted the principles that guided his life—faith, family, and community—Chris was unshaken when the moment of decision came for him to stay by his wife's side rather than return to the Buffalo Bills. Because he had developed a set of rules to live by, Chris was able to demonstrate what had previously been declared: "Now my moment of truth had arrived," he said. "I would serve God, serve my family, and serve the community."[4]

Chris soon received letters from teammates expressing shock that he would give up the game of football. Walking away from a successful career was difficult for the All-Pro linebacker, but Chris never wavered in his decision. Relying on his faith, Chris cared for Stefanie and their four children during her battle with cancer. "The decision didn't call for some great, gallant sacrifice on my part," reflects Chris. "My love for Stef compelled me to do it, and besides, it was just the right thing to do."[5]

Before we can judge our life by solid principles, we have to establish what they are. We need to know what is "the right thing to do," so that when our moment of truth comes, we can make our decision based on those established principles or rules.

Developing Your Values

I grew up loving and playing football. The net effect of this experience is that I understand the game. I know the rules and recognize the signals of the referees. But when it comes to sports like soccer, hockey, or the X Games events, count me out. I don't understand what is going on.

In some ways, people are like the various sports. The exact applications and strategies are different—but the fundamental core values are the same. Regardless of the sport, the essential values behind the penalties and guidelines involve fairness, maximum competition, ethical sportsmanship, scorekeeping, basic safety, and (of course) winning or losing.

For all of us, the essential ground rules are the same. The way we play the game and apply those fundamentals in the practical arena of life may look different. But we still must take the time to decide where the boundaries are, what fairness means, what constitutes a penalty, and what it means to score. So how do you define your rules for the contest of life?

Assessing Your Demonstrated Values

It's been said that an "expert" is anyone, with anything to say, at least fifty miles from home. In other words, if you get far enough from the context in which you live your daily life, and are among folks with whom there is no real accountability, you can act like a know-it-all—and get away with it. The warning here is that we may be impressive to those who don't know us but lack integrity with those who do. This reminds us that our reputation is what people think we are; character is what God knows us to be. The objective is not to be an "expert" when it comes to values. Our aim is to be an example. To that end we must practice a regimen on brutal honesty and ongoing evaluation. At issue here is: "How do I *live* this system of values?"

It's possible to be deceived. The first chapter of James hits us with both barrels when it reminds us: "But prove yourselves doers of the word, and not merely hearers who delude themselves" (v. 22 NASB). A few verses later we read, "If anyone thinks himself to be religious, and yet does not bridle his tongue but deceives his own heart, this man's religion is worthless" (v. 26 NASB). We must constantly make sure that our actions, attitudes, and words are moving in the direction of what we have understood to be right and true.

Again, keep in mind that this is a regular, preferably daily, process. The vulnerability of our heart to conform to the world's system of values is very subtle. In the midst of thousands of daily distractions, our minds can easily drift out of focus in connection to principles that matter the most. We must constantly evaluate: *Am I merely declaring these principles, or does my life demonstrate them?*

Early in His ministry, Jesus was approached one day by Satan, who said to Him, "If You are the Son of God, command that these stones become bread" (Matthew 4:3 NASB). Being tempted in the area of physical appetite after forty days without food, Jesus could have replied, "Yes, I am hungry. I think that's a good idea." Instead, He counteracted the temptation by answering, "It is written, 'Man shall not live on bread alone, but on every word that proceeds out of the mouth of God'" (v. 4 NASB). By quoting from the Law (Deuteronomy 8:3), He declared and demonstrated an integrated value system.

Satan then tried to tempt Him with personal gain by going to the pinnacle of the temple and saying, "Throw Yourself down. For it is written: 'He shall give His angels charge over you,' and 'in their hands they shall bear you up'" (Matthew 4:6). Cunningly using the verse out of context, Satan offered Jesus an opportunity that would have been quite spectacular. Still, Jesus responded, "It is written again, 'You shall not tempt the LORD your God'" (4:7). In effect, Jesus again answered *no* with the knowledge that true gain comes only from doing the will of God.

One more time, when offered the power and glory of all the kingdoms of the world, He was tempted. Declining again, Jesus said, "Be gone, Satan! For it is written, 'You shall worship the Lord your God and him only shall you serve'" (4:10 ESV). He manifested the principle that real power is in worshiping God alone. Anything less is mere emptiness.

Paul understood this as he prayed that the Colossians would embrace God's wisdom and principles and live them out into fruitfulness (1:9–10). To do this requires that we look at the way we are living (1:23, 28). Are we playing by God's rules, or are we being held captive by philosophies that aren't biblical (2:4–10)?

Test One: My Thoughts

Since the Bible clarifies that "as [a man] thinks in his heart, so is he" (Proverbs 23:7) every person must ask himself, "What dominates my thoughts?" The central obsessions of our thought life demonstrate the things that really matter.

Test Two: My Time

In today's world, time has become our most precious commodity and a surefire indicator of our real values. It is easy to declare that issues like family, community service, or physical fitness are important values, but our calendar reveals the true story of what matters most.

Test Three: My Money

You can tell what matters to someone simply by looking at his checking account. The Bible makes it clear that "where your treasure is, there your heart will be also" (Matthew 6:21). Many say something to the effect of, "I love God's kingdom, so I give 1 percent of my income." Here is a disparity, because if you love something you will give it priority. You can't love without giving, without sacrifice, and if He's not first in the financial area of your life, what you demonstrate contradicts your declared philosophy.

Test Four: My Reactions

Here is another question that could help: "How do I react to the unexpected?" Usually a person can calculate behavior in advance, but when unexpectedly forced, one reacts in accordance to what he or she really believes and what really matters. I remember in my high school days being quite intrigued with the writings of Watchman Nee. In a series of practical lectures, he dedicated an entire chapter to the issue of "The Christian Reaction." He essentially stated that you can tell much more about a person's Christianity by their reactions than by their actions.[6]

Although we say we want to be servants, we may revert to pride, self-protection, or even winning at any cost. Gordon MacDonald said it this way: "You can tell whether you're becoming a servant by how you act when people treat you like one."[7] How do I react to the unexpected? This will demonstrate what my real philosophy is.

Test Five: Honest Evaluation from Friends and Relatives

I've heard it said that pride is like bad breath; everyone knows you have it but you! Not only is this true of pride but also of many other qualities in our lives that become blind spots. If you are really serious about getting a read on the values you demonstrate, ask yourself, "What would those who know me best and love me most say is true about me if they knew I could handle it?" Those closest to us don't just hear our words, they see our lives too. They are often in touch with the reality of our actions versus the verbalization of words.

Clarifying Your Declared Values

Now it is time to create alignment between what you demonstrate and what you really want to embrace as the guiding principles of your life. This is done by reflecting on what is important, clarifying those values, then writing them down, and finally organizing them in a way that will spark a deeper and daily renewal that will be woven into the fabric of daily life. The process can incorporate several exercises. The rest of this chapter is an overview. The Values Discovery Exercises (Part Two) will guide you through the process of making application and articulating your values.

The Underpinning of Unchanging Truth

The best values are based on the most reliable truths. The foundation of the Word of God is your starting place. Of the many verses in the sixty-six books of Scripture, you may want to choose themes and key passages that have most influenced you in your personal reading and study. The Values Discovery Exercises start with brainstorming practical principles for living. Be patient and open to the Lord as you do so. This may take many months to formulate your ideas in a careful and applicable way.

This is an exercise done in the same spirit as that mentioned in Deuteronomy 11:18–21, where God told the leaders and fathers of Israel,

> You shall therefore impress these words of mine on your heart and on your soul; and you shall bind them as a sign on your hand, and they shall be as frontals on your forehead. And you shall teach them to your sons, talking of them when you sit in your house and when you walk along the road and when you lie down and when you rise up. You shall write them on the doorposts of your house and on your gates, so that your days and the days of your sons may be multiplied on the land which the LORD swore to your fathers to give them, as long as the heavens remain above the earth.
>
> NASB

The intention here is to remember, practice, and reproduce core values. Keep that in mind as you journey through the process.

Formulations Consistent With Your Foundation

Continue by reviewing your theology, identity, and purposes in life. In order to properly guide these foundational answers, choose the principles that will best guide your journey.

Mentors, Models, and Heroes

Next, who are your mentors, models, or heroes? Some may be biblical, some otherwise historic, while others may be personal acquaintances or family members. For years I had a "wall of faith" in my office: ten pictures that included family members and Christian leaders I've known personally. Under each picture I noted each person's outstanding qualities. I considered them regularly. It has been said that we should cultivate in ourselves the qualities we most admire in others. This is a part of your formulation process.

Seek Honest Feedback

I also suggest asking friends and family members who can be trusted as "truth tellers" to give you feedback on what they see as deeply held qualities and commitments in your life. Add these to your list. Remember, this is a brainstorming process. Let the list grow without much critical evaluation. Eventually you'll do some synthesizing and combining of overlapping qualities.

Refining Your List

As the Values Discovery Exercises will show you, the next step is to prayerfully and carefully identify the most compelling values from the comprehensive list you have compiled. I suggest you choose anywhere from six to a dozen of the most important ones. A one-word description or brief phrase that captures the essence of each quality is your goal. Then write some clarifying sentences behind each one. For future review, keep it clear, condensed, memorable, and meaningful.

Making It Practical

Shortly after I became a father, I felt an urgency to pass on to my children a set of practical ideals they would remember after they grew up and left our home. This aspiration forced me to give my first serious consideration to the task of clarifying values. The result was not profound or pithy, but it helped my children remember some "rules for the game of life."

I ended up drafting a simple set of twelve principles that I clarified and communicated to them in creative ways over the years. Each principle took the form of a little slogan. Over time, I memorized these principles and, for the most part, so did the kids. Back in the day, I gave each of them a three-ring binder, professionally printed, with the full text of the verses. These have become real treasures to them. Today, as adults (and now with their own children) we talk often of our "Twelve Principles." I have a feeling they will be passed on for generations to come (see appendix 10, "The Henderson Family Values").

In attempting to come up with a family philosophy, I think of another family who had just sold their home in the city and moved to the country to raise cattle.

After they were settled in their new location and had bought a large herd, a friend came to visit. Curious, he asked, "What did you finally name this ranch?" The father hesitated, then said, "Well, I wanted to name it The Flying W, but my wife liked The Suzy Q. Our sons suggested The Bar J, and our daughter preferred The Lazy Y. So we call it The Flying W, Suzy Q, Bar J, Lazy Y Ranch." The visitor looked around and then asked, "So, where are the cattle?" The father again hesitated before replying, "None of them survived the branding."

The bottom line is that clear values matter for your own integrity, your relationships, your direction in life, and your ultimate satisfaction and significance. So how do we start the process of clarifying, memorizing, and integrating these values in life in order to satisfy our deep need for clarity and reassurance?

Organize to Memorize

After thinking deeply about your guiding principles, it may be worthwhile to organize them in an easy-to-remember form. I have organized my personal values using the acrostic from my first name. This makes it easy to remember. I try to review it every day and think about it regularly, and am still adding Scriptures and detailed applications to each principle (see appendix 11, "Personal Values").

As Paul wrote to Timothy, "Continue in the things you have learned and become convinced of" (2 Timothy 3:14 NASB). He was instructing this young man in an age when deceivers, evil men, and impostors were going from bad to worse. It, too, was a society in which people had their feet firmly planted in midair. 89

Surrounded by this world view, Paul reminded Timothy to come back to the basic principles that he began learning in infancy. These principles are comprised of the wisdom that leads to salvation through Jesus Christ.

Paul reminded him that "all Scripture is inspired by God and profitable for teaching, for reproof, for correction, for training in righteousness" (2 Timothy 3:16 NASB). God's Word would equip him to stand strong—all the more vital because the day was coming when people would have itching ears, and they would seek teachers who would say whatever they wanted to hear. They also would turn aside to myths, to philosophies that had no moorings. This is why, even today, you need to make clear what you believe, and then keep holding on to it.

Closing the Gap by His Grace

A story is told of two older women who were in an English cemetery that was somewhat crowded with gravesites. They came upon one headstone that read, "Here lies John Smith, a politician and an honest man." One of the women said to the other, "Good heavens! Isn't it awful that they had to bury two people in the same grave!"

My purpose for telling this story is not to pick on politicians, because some are honest. But we need to examine our lives for any disparity now so that passersby won't stumble over the message on our headstone.

Now is the time to bring the authority of truth into your life and subordinate what you do to what you say. Invite the Lord to close the gap. In a disciplined way, constantly subject your mind for renewal in the knowledge of the truth and things already declared important. Commit yourself to those things. As Paul wrote, "Be renewed in the spirit of your mind" (Ephesians 4:23) and "put on the new self who is being renewed to a true knowledge according to the image of the One who created him" (Colossians 3:10 NASB).

When I was growing up, a principle of life in our home was self-honesty, no-excuse living. My parents would often say, "Daniel, you do what you want to do." This would effectively defuse my lame explanations for not doing my chores or homework. Basically, it was a call to look at my heart and see the disparity between my words and my deeds.

This is an essential part of a consistent set of values. It does no good to have an elaborate declaration of values when we have a poor demonstration of them. When what we do contradicts what we say, it is time for a reality check. Either I need to cast myself afresh upon God's grace with a heart of honest repentance or make necessary adjustments in my declared philosophy statement.

The Value of Integrity in Values

Pastor and educator Tony Campolo described an insightful social research poll conducted on fifty people, all over the age of ninety-five. They were asked, "What would you do differently if you had life to live over again?" Their top three answers? I would reflect more, risk more, and do more things that would live on after I'm dead.[8]

A Christian interpretation of this would be, "I would take more time to clarify the principles that really matter. Then, after examining their eternal value, I would take the risk and boldly live out my life based on these principles." Again, this is the collective voice of fifty people with ninety-five-plus years of experience. Still, a person doesn't have to reach this age to learn these lessons.

Those who live meaningful lives are people of deep conviction. To develop conviction you must slow down and ask yourself what matters. Then check and see if there is a disparity between what you say and what you do. In the beginning, it may have to be a daily process. With consistent practice, though, the principles will become clear both in your words and in your life.

The Impact of Our Choices

Bertrand Russell, the Nobel Prize-winning philosopher and mathematician from England, declared himself an atheist in 1890 at the age of eighteen. From then on his "theology," identity, mission, and philosophy made him a topic of controversy around the world. His disdain of God, hatred for Christianity, opposition to war, and inordinate advocacy of loose morality shaped his entire life experience.

Living by these values, he was married four times and had many lovers. Dora, his second wife, was pregnant at the time of their marriage with the first of two children they would conceive. Consistent with his philosophy of life, Russell believed in open marriage. However, after Dora bore two children by another man, Russell could not stand the "torture" of family life and they divorced.

By his fourth marriage, Russell again reaped the fruit of his flawed value system. His son John and John's wife decided they were also tired of family life and separated. They also abandoned their three daughters, and Russell had the responsibility of raising these grandchildren in his later years. John eventually suffered a breakdown.

The bright spot in all of this is the fact that Russell's daughter Kate married an American who became an Episcopal minister. In a dramatic departure from the life-views of her father, Kate and her husband went to Uganda as missionaries.

In his book *What Happened to Their Kids?* Malcolm Forbes surprisingly quotes Kate as crediting her father for her religious conversion. She speaks of the impossible demands of her father, and how, as children, they were "loaded down with inescapable and, to us, inexplicable guilt." As a result, she chose a better theology, identity, purpose, and philosophy.

She did not see her father, one of the most famous atheists of his time, as being entirely irreligious. In looking back on his life, she noted in her memoirs, "I believe myself that his whole life was a search for God; or for those who prefer less personal terms, for absolute certainty."[9]

This sad account reminds us of the lifelong result of fundamental choices. As you choose your "rules to live by," remember the impact your choices will have on your life and on those around you—for better or worse.

A Deeper Life Story

Unexpected storms can be scary. Some leave destruction behind; others cause us to marvel at the awesomeness of God's power. All storms purify the environment and bring life-giving rain.

In our home, we have named our recent storm "Hurricane Lucifer." Although the eye was centered on my husband's job, every area of our lives was affected. I felt as though we were on that boat with the disciples and Jesus was beckoning us to focus on Him, although we were both seasick and deflated from all the stresses of the season of hard work, relationships, and uncertain income.

It was right in the middle of this storm that I began to study the principles in Daniel Henderson's book. God used this study to help me develop a deeper understanding of the fact that there was nothing in my past that was a circumstance, nothing in my present that was occurring outside of His omniscience, and nothing in my future that was impossible for me to attain with the combination of His empowerment and my perseverance. These were all things that I knew but didn't embrace at the onset of my storm. Although I had declared these values, I realized that the time had come to begin demonstrating them.

As an educator, I am very accustomed to making plans for strategic steps toward achieving academic goals for my students. It never occurred to me that this same careful planning when applied to my roles as a wife, mother, and family member would be just as fruitful. I now have a purpose statement: **To demonstrate His love to those in my life.**

Through deep thought and prayer, I have determined my values and established priorities that will carry me through this season of my life. They are to spend time with God, spend time with my husband and two-year-old daughter, and be an excellent teacher, in order to bring Him glory. In our home we have begun implementing "Rules to Live By" using an acrostic from our last name. These rules have helped to anchor us in the midst of our storm. Our boat now feels a little steadier as we commit to living according to our declared values. With fewer distractions in our lives, we can now focus on the Lord as He guides us to a safe harbor.

—Trachide Green, teacher

5

What Shall I Do?

Whatever failures I have known, whatever errors I have committed, whatever follies I have witnessed in private and public life have been the consequence of action without thought.[1]

—Bernard Baruch

A life in which anything goes will ultimately be a life in which nothing goes.[2]

—John Maxwell

My older brother, Dennis, used to have a big sign hanging over his desk during his high school days. In bold black letters, on a white background, it read T-H-I-N-K. Needful, isn't it? I've heard it said that the two most difficult things for anyone to do are to think deeply and to do things in order of their importance.

Too often I have been guilty of shallow, thoughtless action and random daily choices. I suppose all of us need a better understanding of how to order our lives in a considerate and intentional fashion. We would do well to heed the repeated admonition of the prophet Haggai, to "consider" our "ways" (Haggai 1:5, 7).

Thinking About "Not Thinking"

As a kid, I occasionally did stupid things—especially when I forgot to think. For instance, during my early years in Albuquerque, New Mexico, we had a pool in our backyard. That pool attracted many of my neighborhood friends and supplied hours of fun, as long as I was thinking.

One afternoon my parents came home to find my friends and me enjoying ourselves in the pool. Unfortunately, we were not allowed to be in the pool when they were not home. We definitely were not supposed to climb onto the roof of the house and with a running start jump over some electrical wires and land in the deep end of the pool.

Our delight was suddenly interrupted by my mother's horrified screams. How were we to know that we all could have gone to the "swimming pool in the sky" by electrocution? My friends quickly deserted me and left me to face justice alone.

"Danny (my childhood name), what were you thinking?" my parents asked. I could only respond, "I don't know." Mom scolded me with "Danny, sometimes you just don't think," and then Dad applied the "board of education" to my "seat of knowledge."

One other such memory from that same summer involved an exchange with my brother, Dennis. He was about seventeen, and I was six. I was in the pool having a blast, swimming by myself. (My parents had banned my friends from swimming with me by now.) Suddenly he appeared at the back door and announced, "Danny, get out of the pool, the preacher is here." Our pastor had dropped by unexpectedly. Etiquette demanded that I dry off and come in to show my respect. Not wanting to leave the pool so suddenly, I responded with an obscenity. I had no idea what it meant, I just remembered a friend saying it a few times at moments like that. Before I knew it, my very angry brother had me inside, forcing me to take a bite out of a bar of Lava soap. This was apparently some kind of Baptist ritual for ceremonial palate cleansing. Once I had thoroughly chewed up this gritty tidbit (and spat it out), my brother asked, "What were you thinking?"

You know the rest of the story. It became obvious to us all that sometimes I just did not think.

Forty years have passed since those days in and around the pool. I now go by "Daniel." (Only my wife can call me "Danny" and get away with it.) I no longer jump off roofs or chew on Lava soap. But every once in a while I ask myself, *Danny, what were you thinking?*

Too Busy Doing to Think About Doing

Regardless of our stage in life, we never outgrow the need to stop and think, to consider our ways—and then to do things in the order of their importance. This is the essence of a clear understanding of priorities.

Business writer Stephen Covey described our thoughtless ways as an "urgency addiction."[3] He identified this tendency as the habit of finding our security in busyness. The adrenaline rush of hurrying off to handle "important" tasks provides an artificial sense of worth, power, control, and accomplishment.

But over time, without a firm foundation, our real problems worsen, relationships suffer, and we find ourselves unfulfilled. I admit that a sense of urgency taps me on the shoulder every so often. I want to be like Joshua and pray to have God stop the sun for twenty-four hours to finish a task (Joshua 10:1–15). With those precious moments I would think deeply about these essential questions and challenge others to do the same. I would gather everyone around me and say, "All right, now, grab a pencil, paper, and your Bible. In the time that we have, we're going to get on our knees and start asking, thinking about, and answering these questions: *Who is God? Who are you? Why are you here? What really matters to you? Where are you going?* and *What are you going to do about it?*

The Age-Old Addiction

Urgency addiction and misplaced priorities are not new. The story about sisters Martha and Mary gives us an opportunity to hear

Jesus address the problem. It happened when Martha, distracted by all her urgent preparations for their houseguests, said, "Lord, do You not care that my sister has left me to do all the serving alone? Then tell her to help me" (Luke 10:40 NASB).

Jesus replied, "Martha, Martha, you are worried and bothered about so many things; but only one thing is necessary, for Mary has chosen the good part, which shall not be taken away from her" (vv. 41–42 NASB). Where was Mary? She was seated at Jesus' feet, listening to His words. She made the choice to focus on her relationship with Christ and not just react to His visit. Her decision brought eternal perspective and value to the day.

When we take the time to stop and think about our vital choices, as part of an intentional renewal, it makes a fundamental difference. To think deeply about the best priorities may keep us from just running off in the direction of what is merely good. Like Martha, our overloaded life may induce unnecessary frustration, produce a demanding spirit, and even cause us to question God's care.

Like Mary, we can be thoughtful and embrace the few things that are really necessary and the "one thing" of a proper relationship to Christ. It seems she exhibited the fruit of deliberate forethought about the best things. Life is too short and precious for us to do otherwise. Choices matter on earth and last for eternity.

These two sisters represent all of us: people with real struggles, making real choices every day. "What shall I do?" is a question evenly balanced between thinking and doing. First, you must wisely decide, and then incorporate the decision into your lifestyle.

Guarding and Guiding Our Priorities

The practical crucible of life teaches us that we cannot do everything and we certainly cannot please everyone. The nature of society's increasing array of choices pulls us in many directions at once. The needs of people around us compel us to respond to more expectations than we can possibly bear. That is why we need clear priorities.

I define priorities as the commitments we put first in our lives because we believe they are important. The key term here is *commitments*. This resolve is distinguished from the act of *prioritizing*, which is a simple function of time management and ordering daily tasks. Instead, we are addressing the basic areas of one's life-focus—the commitments to which we dedicate large portions of our time. These commitments ultimately determine our goals and the way we spend our time.

Some years ago, three hundred whales died after becoming marooned in a bay. They became trapped while pursuing sardines. One commentator observed, "The small fish lured the giants to their death. They came to their violent demise by chasing small ends, by prostituting vast powers for insignificant goals."[4]

Like these giant mammals, the vast power of God's Spirit in the lives of believers is often prostituted when we chase things that are ultimately insignificant. If only we would think and do things that are ultimately important.

The problem with priorities is not "out there." It's not the boss, family, our schedule, or any other person. The priority issue begins inside each one of us; then, if successful, it becomes visible through our daily actions. I believe we face three major obstacles that keep our priorities from coming to fruition in our lives.

Lack of Integration: Priorities Are Displaced by Unimportant Things

The first obstacle is allowing unimportant things to displace our priorities. Not every choice is of equal importance in time and in eternity. Without a solid foundation of truth, our determinations may be skewed by subjectivity. We may reflect the conviction expressed by the sign on one businessman's desk: "My decision is maybe, and that's final."

As one writer described it: "If you're going to pull decisions out of a hat, make sure you're wearing the right hat."[5] If we fail to integrate our priorities with clear values that frame a biblical life purpose, as an expression of our identity, founded on our theology, then we're just pulling our priorities out of a hat.

Lack of Preparation: Priorities Are Displaced by Urgent Things

A second obstacle to be aware of is an internal lack of preparation. This is where priorities are displaced by seemingly urgent things. Former President Dwight D. Eisenhower has been credited with saying, "The urgent is seldom important, and the important is seldom urgent."

This was brought home years ago in a tragic way when the now defunct Eastern Airlines' flight 401 crashed between New York and Miami. As the crew prepared to land, they noticed that a light to indicate the landing gear was down had failed to respond. They weren't sure if the problem was the light or the landing gear. The flight engineer attempted to remove the bulb, but it wouldn't loosen. Other members of the crew tried to help him. As they struggled with the bulb, no one noticed the plane was losing altitude. It crashed into a swamp and people died. This experienced crew of highly trained technicians and pilots became preoccupied with an inexpensive light bulb and a plane full of passengers became tragic casualties.[6]

All of us are on a lifetime trip. If we don't take time to prepare our hearts and thoughts according to an integrated foundation of truth, we will constantly be displacing things that matter with the less important things that surprise us with their urgency every day of life.

Lack of Conviction: Priorities Are Displaced by Unplanned Things

The third obstacle to watch for is a lack of conviction. This is where the unplanned things displace priorities. We may have clarified our priorities and endeavored to integrate them into our lifestyles, but if we lack conviction, the internal decisions will never see the light of day.

Unplanned obstacles usually come in the form of people. One leader in a church where I served would remind me that *no* is a Christian word. It is not an easy expression, but it is an essential one. Sometimes you have to decline the invitation to distraction, because well-meaning people living in a crisis mode are prone to request that you change your plans in order to fulfill theirs. But, as the saying goes, "A lack of planning on your part does not constitute an emergency on my part."

A mentor early in my ministry often said, "The power of *no* is in a stronger *yes.*" If we have not clearly embraced the yes commitments of solid priorities, we will be subjected to unimportant, urgent, and unplanned influences to our own demise, affecting our fruitfulness for Christ and relationships with others.

This is like the old lighthouse keeper who worked on a rocky stretch of coastline. Every month he would receive a new supply of oil to keep the light burning. Because he was near the shore, he had frequent guests. One night a woman came from a nearby village and begged for some oil to keep her family warm. Another time a father asked for some to use in his lamp.

Someone else needed oil to lubricate a wheel. All of these requests sounded legitimate, so the lighthouse keeper granted the requests. Toward the end of the month, he noticed that his supply of oil was very low. Soon it was gone, and the beacon went out. That night, several ships were wrecked and lives were lost. When the authorities investigated, the man was very repentant. Yet through all his excuses and pleading, the investigators told him, "You were given oil for one purpose: to keep the light burning."[7] This was their conviction. It had failed to be his.

God has given us a theology, an identity, a purpose, and a philosophy for a reason: They help us identify the priorities that matter to Him. We need to strengthen our conviction to live for Him, even when other people may not understand our *no.* Their crises will usually seem very important, yet even these will require decisions based upon strong convictions.

Clarifying and Communicating Our Commitments

In my years as pastor, I often had to draw upon a strong conviction about what I should be doing when responding to many personal requests and countless expectations. Through a prayerful and deliberate process, I was able to focus my service to Christ and the church around five very specific priorities (see appendix 12, "Five Ministry Priorities"). I reviewed and reaffirmed these priorities almost every morning. I explained them regularly to my staff and our board. I shared them with my wife and family, soliciting prayer support for my effectiveness in implementing these essential commitments. I even communicated them to the church at least once a year, explaining why each was vital and biblical. This helped the congregation understand why these commitments would best serve the needs of the people.

As I sought to live out these compelling priorities, I sometimes needed to use that Christian word *no*. When deciding my daily schedule, these clear commitments provided a firm foundation for specific goals and corollary time management.

One point should be made before we proceed with selecting priorities. This suggested exercise in the next section needs to be executed at least annually because the deeper the process, the more dynamic the issues become. Our theology will not change drastically, except as our understanding of biblical truth grows. Identity, once based on truth, will remain intact—as will our purposes. Occasionally our guiding principles may need to be adjusted. However, because of the dynamic nature of our priorities, it is wise to evaluate them on a regular basis.

Determining Priorities: Six Guideposts

As you exercise your mind to think about the priorities that merit your primary attention, it is important to utilize objective criteria in the process. Here are six guideposts to watch for.

Scripture—Because Truth Is the Basis of Our Commitments

The ultimate guidepost is *Scripture*: "Oh, that my steps might be steady, keeping to the course you set; then I'd never have any regrets in comparing my life with your counsel" (Psalm 119:5–6 MESSAGE). The Word of God must determine our areas of primary concentration. When truth is our guide, we avoid regrets.

What is God's counsel? The bulk of His counsel about priorities is found in this passage:

> Jesus said . . . "You shall love the LORD your God with all your heart, with all your soul, and with all your mind." This is the first and great commandment. And the second is like it: "You shall love your neighbor as yourself." On these two commandments hang all the Law and the Prophets.
>
> Matthew 22:37–40

Is this counsel guiding your priority choices? Is your life, first and foremost, motivated by love? When love is the motive, relationships are the means through which these priorities are expressed. Jesus says that the first priorities in life are relational, starting with your relationship with God, then with family, friends, and others. Dying people never say that they wish they had spent more time shuffling papers at the office or playing video games. What really matters is relationships. Jesus makes it clear. This is *A*, this is *B*, and everything else falls behind these priorities.

Stewardship—Because We Are Accountable to God for Our Commitments

The second guidepost is *stewardship*. The apostle Peter said, "As each one has received a special gift, employ it in serving one another as good stewards of the manifold grace of God" (1 Peter 4:10 NASB). Likewise, Paul said, "It is required of stewards that one be found trustworthy" (1 Corinthians 4:2 NASB). Every member of Christ's body, by the grace of God, has been equipped to minister. It may help to ask: "What can only I do, versus what others can do?" The answer will influence your life-management decisions.

Business writers offer this advice: "Get into the habit of asking yourself if someone else can handle what you're doing." A clear-thinking person lets go so that others can do some of the tasks that are perhaps being neglected. They will do them well, and probably better than you. It's one of the benefits of teamwork. Teamwork is certainly necessary in the home, in business, and in ministry. It may be risky to allow another person to fulfill someone's request, because it can result in disappointment. I know that I often disappoint people in our church. I don't want to, but I have to if I am going to live by my priorities. It's what counselors call "setting boundaries." At the end of the Priorities Discovery Exercises is a chart that I have found useful in evaluating commitments.

As I led large congregations over the years, I came to realize that I can't keep everyone's "hope alive" when it comes to how I spend my life. Long ago, I learned that twenty-five years in the future I may be just a framed photo in the church lobby. People who know me will recognize the picture, while children will run by thinking, "Who's that old guy?" Some new pastor will be leading the ministry, proving that I was indeed expendable. But twenty-five years from now, I will still be the only father my children have ever known. No one else in the whole world can fill that role for them. I have a unique stewardship in being their father. This realization is enough to help me choose priorities.

Servanthood—Because We Are Called to Love Others Through Our Commitments

The third guidepost is *servanthood*. Jesus said, "Whoever wishes to be first among you shall be slave of all. For even the Son of Man did not come to be served, but to serve, and to give His life a ransom for many" (Mark 10:44–45 NASB).

What priorities would be of most benefit to the people I am called to serve? Of all the choices, what will best serve my family? What will best serve the body of Christ? Sometimes I have to consider not only individuals but also the whole gathering. One of my pastoral priorities was always to protect significant and uninterrupted study time. For the sake of the entire flock, this was essential to my primary duties of preaching and leadership.

Occasionally someone would drift into the offices on a study day, not understanding why I did not take the time to chat. To do so would have violated, for the sake of one inquirer, my stewardship to an entire congregation. Of course, in crisis situations I made exceptions. We all must come to terms with how we can best order our lives to benefit those we are called to serve.

Significance—Because Not All Commitments Have Equal Eternal Value

Another guidepost is *significance*. What priorities will matter in eternity? Which will benefit God's work the most and have the greatest impact on God's kingdom? The apostle Paul said, "We look not at the things which are seen, but at the things which are not seen; for the things which are seen are temporal, but the things which are not seen are eternal" (2 Corinthians 4:18 NASB). Are my life priorities based on the seen or the unseen? Which is truly significant?

For parents, raising successful children is a priority. Many choose to involve their children in sports in order to help build confidence and self-esteem. An estimated thirty-five million children in the U.S. participate in organized sports each year.[8] While the benefits of sports are many, well-intentioned parents can soon find themselves entrapped by the demands of too many commitments. The term *soccer mom* came into widespread use in the late nineties as a way to describe the "overburdened middle-income working mother who ferries her kids from soccer practice to scouts to school."[9] Overburdened and overcommitted moms (and dads) soon feel the pressure of producing star performers. Statistics show that 70 percent of children will drop out of team sports before turning thirteen. The biggest reason? Parental pressure. A Michigan State Youth Institute survey cited "adults, particularly parents" as the reason for the high dropout rate, saying that the game became a "joyless, negative experience" for the children.[10]

Reflecting on the appropriate priorities of a parent as described in Proverbs 22:6—"Train up a child in the way he should go, and when he is old he will not turn from it"—Lysa TerKeurst wrote, "I am challenged to ponder these words, 'in the way he should go.' Are we training our kids that 'the way he should go' is to chase worldly achievement or to chase God? Whatever they learn to chase as a child, they will chase as adults. Therefore, we must be challenged to honestly assess the way we are pointing them to go."[11]

Our priorities determine how we spend our time and demonstrate what we consider significant. Clearly the Bible teaches that this visible world is passing away. If a person makes choices based upon this temporal input, the results are not going to last. Again, sports offer many benefits in a child's life, but winning the championship trophy in and of itself does not accomplish much that counts in eternity.

Paul wrote, "I have fought the good fight, I have finished the course, I have kept the faith; in the future there is laid up for me the crown of righteousness, which the Lord, the righteous Judge, will award to me on that day; and not only to me, but also to all who have loved His appearing" (2 Timothy 4:7–8). Here is a man who ran the course of life with his choices based on the unseen.

Satisfaction—Because We Enjoy Good Rewards in Keeping Vital Commitments

The fifth guidepost is *satisfaction.* Jesus said to His disciples, "My food is to do the will of Him who sent Me and to accomplish His work" (John 4:34 NASB). Every true Christ-follower finds great joy in obedience and genuine discipleship. This is the mark of a truly converted and surrendered heart.

Beyond this, every one of us exhibits a unique God-given design (as we saw in chapter 2, "Who Am I?"). Part of this design is reflected in the pursuits that we find genuinely satisfying. My daughter finds satisfaction in giving a great "cut and color" in her career as a hair stylist. She also feels deep joy when she completes a painting. This is evidence of God's design leading to satisfaction upon completing an enjoyable task.

My wife finds satisfaction in completing a decorating project or serving a delicious meal. One son is overjoyed when he harvests an eight-point buck. The other is elated when he can solve a mechanical problem or create a video project. I find satisfaction in seeing the "lights come on" when I am speaking on a particular subject.

The goal for each of us, when all is said and done, is the personal satisfaction of knowing our choice is pleasing to God and fulfills our hearts by God's design.

Stability—Because Our Commitments Provide Essential Boundaries and Balance

The sixth and final guidepost when considering our priorities is *stability*. Our lives consist of balancing many things in a limited amount of time. We must consider job, family, service, sleep, and leisure, to name just a few. And let's not forget eating and rest. Jesus didn't. After an intense period of ministry, He said to His disciples, "'Come away by yourselves to a secluded place and rest a while.' For there were many people coming and going, and they did not even have time to eat" (Mark 6:31). Jesus helped His disciples keep their priorities straight.

Many of us have seen lion trainers at the circus. They always have whips and often a gun. I've never seen one without a stool. I've wondered if they think that little stool is going to have any deterring effect on that large lion when they point the legs toward the growling beast. Well, those who seem to know say that the animal will try to focus on all four legs at once. This results in a kind of paralysis that overwhelms the ferocious cat and it becomes tame, weak, and disabled. Its attention is fragmented.

Do you have too many "stool legs" in your life? I often tell church leaders that the enemy does not have to destroy us, he simply has to distract us. Too many priorities and too few truly significant commitments can discourage our hearts and dilute our influence in rapid fashion.

Priority Choices Make All the Difference

The power of a focused life is the kind of existence the world is waiting to see. If you adequately answer the question "What shall I do?" you will stop chasing sardines into the bay like a hungry whale. Little fish lose their appeal when we see that Scripture clearly guides choices that empower our journey as a steward and a servant. This results in significance and satisfaction, which in turn leads to a stable, well-rounded life.

C. S. Lewis said, "If you put first things first, the second things will get thrown in. But if you put second things first, then you lose both first and second."[12] Jesus said, "Seek first His kingdom and His righteousness, and all these things shall be added to you" (Matthew 6:33). Now here is a life-management method that really brings some lasting results. It's sad to see that many people who claim to be Christians fail to follow this time-tested approach. As a consequence, the enemy keeps us distracted and detached from the commitments that really matter.

Robert Frost wrote a classic poem about choosing between two roads. Using the illustration of a walk in the woods, he captured the greater reality of the lasting impact of our choices and commitments. Like the traveler who has to choose between two equally attractive roads that "diverge in a yellow wood," we must make decisions about priorities. As the years pass, our choices make all the difference.

Every day brings many roads to travel. The question will always be, "What should I do?" We must think deeply about what really matters as we reflect on our theology, identity, purpose, and values. Then we must make commitments to the important things. This is a life of intentionality, integrity, and impact. And may it be that we will never have to look our Lord in the face on that day when His pleasure will be all that matters, and hear Him say, "What were you thinking?"

A Deeper Life Story

As a young wife and mother, trying to balance the ever-increasing responsibilities of my various roles often left me feeling like I was hanging by a thread. It seemed like with daily interruptions the important things I wanted to accomplish kept getting postponed. I eventually discovered that I was struggling with every area of my life because I was not committed to spending time daily in God's

Word and in prayer. Daniel Henderson describes the need to use the word **no** as we seek to live out our priorities.

My first focus was to make my spiritual foundation a firm priority. Then I discovered that my relationship with my husband and with my children were to be top priorities as well. Not just caring for my family and our home but also spending quality time building relationships with those I loved. Therefore, prior to committing to new activities or responsibilities, including ministry and volunteer opportunities, I began prayerfully considering how these would impact my time with my family. Saying no was difficult but ultimately necessary.

Shortly after committing to these priorities in my life, I became extremely ill. I was eventually diagnosed with postural orthostatic tachycardia syndrome, a serious chronic illness affecting my heart and severely limiting my physical abilities. My active lifestyle was suddenly slowed down. Meeting even the basic needs of my family became a daily challenge. I was unable to complete the simplest daily tasks, such as driving my daughters to the library or the park. I could no long carry grocery bags or lift a basket of laundry. Putting first things first became an immediate necessity in our home. We were forced to focus on specific priorities each day.

God assures us in 2 Corinthians 12:9 that His power is made perfect in weakness. Acknowledging my weakness, I continue to put my trust in Him, recognizing the importance of beginning each day reading His Word and praying that He will direct my path. I am thankful that these priorities were established in my life prior to the onset of my illness. They kept me from feeling completely overwhelmed when fears of inadequacy threatened to rob me of my purpose as a wife and mother. In addition to bringing balance to our life and home, living out my priorities allows me to focus on the truly important things in my roles of wife and mother and to minister to others according to the will of God.

—Jaime Hammond, housewife and mother

6

How Shall I Do It?

The world stands aside to let anyone pass who
knows where he is going.

—*David Staff Gordon*

Give me a stock clerk with a goal and I will give
you a man who will make history. Give me a man
without a goal and I will give you a stock clerk.

—*J. C. Penney*

Be not afraid of going slowly; be only afraid of
standing still.

—*Chinese proverb*

*S*uccess. *Fulfillment. Winning. Completion. Reward. Satisfaction.* These words, so common in our society, all reflect a
longing in every human soul to accomplish something of significance. It is one thing to aspire to do something of worth. Dreams
are free. Achievement, however, is costly.

Resounding in the soul of every person is the need to accomplish.
Children love to win their childhood games on the playground or
build the best Lego design. Students strive for outstanding grades
on their report cards. Young entrepreneurs work feverishly for their

first profitable year. Mothers labor to raise a child who demonstrates character, good manners, and a sense of direction in life. Dads set their sights on a comfortable retirement and sizeable inheritance for their children. At the end of the journey, we all want to feel like we have achieved something of significance.

Business leaders, life coaches, and personal trainers have agreed that the essential factor in all achievement is good goals. We've been taught that goal-setting enables us to accomplish our dreams and fulfill our resolutions. In fact, goal-setting is described as the fuel that flames meaningful forward progress.

Racing Toward the Goal

The New Testament often compares the Christian life to a contest, or, more specifically, to a race. In Hebrews 12, the victorious racer runs with endurance, laying aside everything that hinders, fixing his eyes on the goal. The writer refers to a runner whose eyes are fixed on a square pillar located at the finish of the race. For Christians, that goal is Jesus.

Paul frequently used the example of running. To the church in Galatia, he said he wanted to run in a way that would not be vain or meaningless (Galatians 2:2).

There certainly wasn't anything meaningless about a race run by a Guatemalan ministry. Rising up the side of a mountain in Zacapa, Guatemala, is a staircase of 250 steps. It is located at Hope of Life, a ministry dedicated to serving the poor throughout the country. The steps were constructed in order to assist the staff in getting quickly from one area of the campus to another. On the day the steps were completed, ministry founder Carlos Vargas held a contest for any staff members willing to race up the steps. Cash prizes were promised to the three runners who could reach the top first.

Among the ten contestants was a sixty-year-old man weighing 200 pounds. The remaining runners were between the ages of fifteen and twenty. Although all the runners took off at the starting pistol, the group soon spread out as some fell behind. The sixty-year-old was among the leaders throughout the race. After finishing in second place, the older runner immediately lost consciousness. He received oxygen and water and then was asked why he risked his life to run against the younger men. "I ran because I needed to win the prize," he said. "I have a daughter, and she is going to die unless she has an operation. I need the prize money to pay for her surgery."[1]

Paul describes how we must fight, work, and strain with purpose, direction, and discipline. In Philippians 3, he focuses on running and finishing the race in order to win the prize that God promised him, the high calling of Jesus Christ. In New Testament times, chariot races were held in many cities of the Roman Empire. Paul may have pictured himself as a charioteer as he described a decisive moment of the race when he strained forward to what lay ahead. Intensely pressing toward the goal of the prize at a high speed, Paul notes that even one glance backward could be tragic and perhaps even fatal in this race. He realized that Christians must forget what they've achieved in the past and must with newly bestowed grace strain forward with all their might.

In these races, judges would sit by the goal, carefully prepared to render their final decision. In a letter to Timothy, Paul wrote, "There is laid up for me the crown of righteousness, which the Lord, the righteous Judge, will award me in that day; and not only to me, but also to all who have loved His appearing" (2 Timothy 4:8 NASB). This kind of race and reward demands our all.

Paul's ultimate long-range life goal was to become like Christ and finish the ministry that God had given him. Along the way Paul established many short-term objectives, plans, and goals.

Writers of today's business literature occasionally overuse the word *goals*. This word has become repulsive to some Christians; they may perceive it as unbiblical. While understandable, it is somewhat reactionary. It may help to establish a working definition of the term.

Goals—The Good and the Bad

The word *goal* originally meant "pole, rod, or stick." Historically, *goal* has meant something visible that would be positioned at the end of a racecourse so that all participants could keep their eyes on the rod or pole. When this word is used, it signifies a point that has been set as a boundary or finishing point.

In Greek the word is *scopos*, from which we get the word *scope*. It represents a mark on which someone would fix their eyes. From these two definitions I've developed this working model: A goal is a mark toward which you direct your life so that you can accomplish your priority commitments and live with integrity.

After we clarify our priorities and come to valid conclusions about what really matters, we take the next step of establishing specific marks, or targets. It's these marks that we set our eyes on, in an all-out effort to see our priorities become reality.

But is goal-setting biblical? The answer is yes and no. It all depends, because a goal is like a rung on a ladder. Whether the goal is good or not depends on the rest of the ladder. It depends on the focus and foundation. It depends on the ground upon which the ladder is resting and the wall against which it is leaning. It may help to have some examples of bad versus good goals.

Biblical Examples of a Bad Approach to Goals

An example of a poor objective is the Tower of Babel in Genesis 11:4. The people basically said, "We want to build for ourselves a city and a tower so that we can reach heaven and build for ourselves a name." In response to their goal, God scattered them and confused their language so that they could not understand one another (v. 7). He had put within them the potential of imagination, creativity, and teamwork, yet they had chosen a bad goal.

Another example is the self-sufficient king in Jeremiah 22:13–14. He purposed to build a large and impressive dwelling in a manner that took advantage of his neighbors by not paying them for their work. The goal was bad and the results were worse.

Then there is King Nebuchadnezzar in Daniel 4:28–36. One day he was on the rooftop of his palace, looking at his great kingdom. He thought, *Look what I have done in building this residence by my power and for my glory*. God, in effect, said, "Bad goal,

Nebuchadnezzar," and this king found himself acting like an animal, with long hair and fingernails, eating grass in the field. This behavior continued until he learned how to choose good goals instead of bad ones.

The New Testament has numerous examples of bad goals. One is the parable of the rich fool of Luke 12. He must have had too much time on his hands and was looking for something to do. He decided to tear down his old barns and build bigger ones for storing all his goods and wealth. Then he could say to his soul, "Eat, drink, and be merry." In response to this goal, God declared him a fool. He, in effect, said, "You're poor toward Me. You may be rich, but your goals and thoughts are way off base. The ladder you're climbing is on the wrong foundation and it's propped against the wrong wall."

Another example is found in James 4:

> Come now, you who say, "Today or tomorrow, we shall go to such and such a city, and spend a year there and engage in business and make a profit." Yet you do not know what your life will be like tomorrow. You are just a vapor that appears for a little while and then vanishes away. Instead, you ought to say, "If the Lord wills, we shall live and also do this or that." But as it is, you boast in your arrogance; all such boasting is evil. Therefore, to one who knows the right thing to do, and does not do it, to him it is sin.
>
> vv. 13–17 NASB

Now these people had appropriate short-term plans. They also had planned long-term for the next year. They had a city in mind, and a particular objective for making money. James didn't say that was bad. He said, "You ought to say, 'If the Lord wills. . . . '" He also pointed out that they were planning out of arrogance, self-will, and selfish desire. The problem in this as in other examples is not that they had goals. The complication comes when the goal is motivated by a wrong heart and finite objective.

God acknowledges that man will have many plans, "Nevertheless the LORD's counsel—that will stand" (Proverbs 19:21). Plans are not wrong. Many people in the Bible had plans, but remember this: 115

It is only the counsel of the Lord that will stand. And that brings us to some examples of good goals.

Biblical Examples of a Good Approach to Goals

We'll start in the Old Testament with Noah's goal of building an ark. God gave Noah a plan. The dimensions were specific, measurable, and attainable. Of course, the task was formidable, yet Noah set about to faithfully obey God. God also gave him a time frame and the reason behind the project. Noah understood that God was going to establish His righteousness on earth, and He was going to do it specifically through Noah and his family.

God was also very specific in telling Moses to build the tabernacle. The instructions included the materials, the people, the timing, and more. With Joshua, God gave specific goals for entering the Promised Land, city by city. Solomon, when given the vision of building the temple, received very specific instructions as well.

In the book of Nehemiah, God gave the long-term goal of rebuilding the wall of Jerusalem. In response, Nehemiah made this goal the priority of his life. He began this task by accomplishing short-term goals. First, he had to get permission from the king. He became accountable by telling the king that, if granted permission, he planned to do it in a certain amount of time. Then he began to survey and plan, to find the right people, to provide motivation, and to deal with opposition. Nehemiah is a wonderful example of setting the right kind of goals.

In the New Testament, I think the best example of good goal-setting is Jesus Christ. Even though the Bible is not specific about His goals, we can learn valuable lessons from His life. At the end of Jesus' ministry He prayed, "I have glorified You on the earth. I have finished the work which You have given Me to do" (John 17:4). Jesus never turned from His commitment to His goals and plans that fulfilled His mission.

Take, for example, His wilderness experience. He didn't just start out walking and then decide to stay for forty days without eating. Rather, it was by design. It was a specific step toward a mark. As was His baptism by John.

And what about the selection of the twelve disciples? Why not choose ten or eighteen? Because there was a plan formed in ages past. Specific events needed to occur. These events had a design, a timetable, an order, and an objective.

Jesus went to the cross at a predetermined time. He was buried, and He rose from the grave on the third day, just as He had predicted. All of this happened by design, in order to accomplish the ultimate goal of redemption. He, being God, fulfilled many measurable segments of this long-range plan. Because we are not God, we need to plan and implement with great dependence upon Him, His Word, and His truth.

Paul knew this as he sought guidance for his life, actions, and travel plans. He wrote, "Now I do not want you to be unaware, brethren, that I often planned to come to you (but was hindered until now), that I might have some fruit among you also" (Romans 1:13). Paul had plans, but he also depended upon God. He said, "Always in my prayers, making request if, by some means, now at last I may find a way in the will of God to come to you" (vv. 9–10).

The Process of Establishing Goals

With these examples in mind, let's move to the actual process of establishing goals. The biblical analogy of a race works well as a framework. Blending experiences of running track with the scriptural picture of a race, the Goals Discovery Exercises (Part Two) will walk you through a six-step goal-setting process: consecration, preparation, imagination, execution, evaluation, and celebration. Before you begin, though, I hope these insights will help.

Step One: Consecration

A successful track season, and effective completion of each race, begins with *consecration*. To run with excellence, you must decide   117 on absolute commitment to the season and its rigors. This means setting aside any distractions and hindrances that are not consistent with top conditioning. Every year during track season, my lifestyle changed as I traded Twinkies for the healthy stuff. Instead of late-night goofing off, I was careful to get adequate rest. I traded afternoon television for healthy workouts. This took consecration and commitment.

When it comes to goals, we must continually give our hearts to God and discard meaningless and temporal ambitions. We must submit our plans to the Lord to confirm that our goals are the same as His.

Not all goals are God-given. People can become very temporal when the time comes for serious goal-setting. When I was in college, I read some information about life planning and became motivated to write three pages of goals. Over the years, I have misplaced those pages, but I do remember a few of my intentions. A major one was to own a herd of buffalo by the time I was thirty. I had always been intrigued by the great American frontiersmen, so I thought this would be a good thing to pursue. Of course, at that age I did not understand that goals should be integrated with a biblical foundation for life.

We often miss the mark when it comes to what our goals should be. I recently came across a hypothetical story of Jesus taking His disciples up to a mountain in order to teach some aspects of the Sermon on the Mount.

> "Blessed are the meek, blessed are those who mourn, blessed are the merciful, blessed are you when you are persecuted," He instructed. "Blessed are you when you suffer. Be glad and rejoice for great is your reward in heaven." Simon Peter then asked, "Are we supposed to know this?" Andrew said, "Do we have to write this down?" James wanted to know if they were going to be tested on the material. Philip didn't have anything to write on, and on it goes with the other disciples. Then one of the Pharisees, asking to see the lesson plan, inquired, "Where is your set of anticipatory goals and objectives in the cognitive domain?" The scene closes with these words: "And Jesus wept."[2]

Sometimes we get wrapped up in tangible, temporal things. We really don't understand the biblical perspective of goals, so we dash off to round up a herd of buffalo. Goals can be biblical. God wants us to make commitments that are specific, accountable, and measurable in fulfilling His will.

With a clear and practical theology shaping our identity and motivating our purposes, we have a strong foundation and framework. Knowing our values and the best priorities to pursue sets us up for specific action. Now it is time to consecrate our hearts and minds to the Lord in order to chart the specific next steps for moving forward.

In college, my priority was to become an effective pastor. Then I decided that a good goal would be to plant a church. Now the pressure began. Specifically, a small group of us decided to plant a church in the Pacific Northwest. This added a little more pressure. Then we decided we were going to do it by a certain time, and this resulted in a greater consecration. But as we established those goals, dates, and specific strategies, God moved and provided in ways that were phenomenal. As people understood our goals and began believing in our vision and commitment, they provided funds to help begin the new church. By the time we moved across the country, we had received the fifty thousand dollars (a lot of money at that time) necessary to move nine households of people committed to planting a church in the Pacific Northwest.

This very first ministry experience became an amazing illustration of the power of specific commitment. God showed himself strong on behalf of those who, based upon the call of God, were willing to act in specific ways. That is what Paul referred to when he spoke of intensity, commitment, and urgency.

Proverbs 16:1–3 says, "The preparations of the heart belong to man, but the answer of the tongue is from the LORD. All the ways of a man are pure in his own eyes, but the LORD weighs the spirits. Commit your works to the LORD, and your thoughts will be established."

Clearly God expects us, and has wired us, to make plans. Our motives may or may not be pure. God knows. He will reveal that to us as we commit our plans to Him. With the illumination of His Word, His Spirit, and wise counsel, we find our thoughts and plans becoming clearer or being redirected. The key is that we commit our works to Him, surrendering to His guidance and trusting in His provision. In time, our thoughts will be established.

Step Two: Preparation

A second major step in the process of establishing goals is *preparation*. In running track, it's the issue of making certain you are ready for the race. How's my energy? Have I warmed up sufficiently? Am I mentally prepared? Is my equipment in good shape? Do I fully understand the distance or duration of this contest?

In order to prepare for establishing goals, we must understand the nature of good goals. When these dynamics are understood, then we are ready to become specific.

The traditional description of good goal-setting is captured in the acrostic SMART (specific, measurable, achievable, relevant, and time-based). Whether short- or long-range, effective goals must provide a *specific* target. Being determined to get healthier is a good intention, even a priority, but it is not a goal until it is *measurable* (e.g., a specific weight, pant size, or cholesterol level). Just like any athletic competition, there must be a scoreboard or a time-to-beat in order to evaluate progress.

Our goals must be *achievable*. I could set a goal to swim the English Channel in record time, but at my age and given my lack of real passion for that exploit, it is not realistic. We are wise to set goals we can achieve, even if later we set a new goal that moves us further ahead. This is why short-term goals are an integral part of long-term goals. As we meet each short-term goal, we become increasingly hopeful of reaching the distant target.

The best goals are *relevant*. Specifically, they must relate to and achieve our established priorities. Otherwise, an irrelevant goal becomes a distraction and dissipation of energy. Goals fulfill priorities—in keeping with our values, in fulfillment of our purpose, as an expression of our identity, and built on a solid theology. Do you sense a repeated progression here?

Good goals must be *time-based*. A "someday" goal is just a wish that enables our complacency. A time target makes us accountable and allows us to pace our measurements as we move ahead.

Step Three: Imagination

Every serious runner thinks ahead and rehearses the race before it begins. He envisions his start out of the blocks, imagines the turns of the track, and dreams of a solid finish.

The holy use of the *imagination* is an important function. It enables us to understand the accomplishment of the goal through the eyes of faith. This hopeful expectation of accomplishment helps us as we prepare to act upon those things God has placed upon our hearts.

A few decades ago, Karl Wallenda, the famous tightrope artist, died after falling from a rigging tied seventy-five feet above the ground.

His wife, who was also an aerialist, had an interesting observation about his actions before the fatal fall. She said, "All Karl thought about for three straight months was trying not to fall. He kept thinking about falling. It was the first time he'd ever thought about that, and it seemed to me that he'd put all his energies into not falling rather than in walking the tightrope." She added that her husband went so far as to personally supervise the installation of that particular tightrope, making absolutely certain the guy wires were secure. Before, he'd always trusted his crew to do this.[3]

We need to trust God. Our focus should not be on failing but on the vision He has for our lives. The reality of what He can do should keep us steady on the tightrope of life.

When Noah had a goal, he could build an ark that offered salvation from the flood. When he lost his vision, he got drunk. Saul's goal was to conquer kings. He lost his focus and couldn't conquer his own jealousy of David. When David imagined God's power at work, he conquered Goliath. When he lost his faith, he couldn't overcome his own lust. Solomon had goals and hopeful expectations of being the wisest man in the world. When he lost what God had given him, he couldn't control his own obsession for foreign women. When Samson had a clear focus, he won many battles; when he lost it, he failed to win his battle with Delilah. Elijah's goal was to pray down fire from heaven. It ended when he ran in despair from Jezebel.

It is the hopeful imagination—the sense that God is doing something—that gives direction for our energies. Good goals motivate us to keep going on in faith. God is constantly stretching us forward to new targets, new avenues for doing His will. Are you feeling stretched?

Step Four: Execution

A popular motivational quote describes the *execution* of goals this way: "Every morning in Africa, a gazelle wakes up. It knows it must run faster than the fastest lion or it will be killed. Every morning a lion wakes up. It knows it must outrun the slowest gazelle or it will starve to death. It doesn't matter whether you are a lion or a gazelle: when the sun comes up, you'd better be running."[4]

When the starting gun goes off, every ounce of your being must be into the effort of the race. The same thing happens in the execution of good goals, when you carefully and prayerfully write them down. Execution is an everyday kind of thing. Keep them easily available, as they are a key component in your daily time of personal spiritual renewal. They will become building blocks to a life where everything fits together.

Step Five: Evaluation

In a race, *evaluation* is essential. This is done with split-second analysis. You examine your pace, assess other runners, keep in your designated lane, monitor breathing, adjust posture, and, straining forward with all your energy, focus on the finish line.

When implementing a goal, evaluate the following: Am I staying focused? What distractions and hindrances do I need to be aware of? What are my time deadlines and how am I doing in meeting these? All during this procedure, pray about these things, commit them to God, and trust Him for the grace to arrive at this worth-while finish line.

It's best to double-check and confirm that your understanding of God's plan is based on the right foundation. In Philippians 3:7, Paul talked about making a confirmation and correction in his foundation. He wrote, "But what things were gain to me, these I have counted loss for Christ." Paul's goal of being a respected Pharisee, a Hebrew of the Hebrews, zealous for what he thought was right, all changed when he encountered Jesus. Everything he thought was important became as dung compared to the riches he found in Him. In verse 14, he said, "I press on toward the goal for the prize of the upward call of God in Christ Jesus." He traded his past goals, ambitions, and aspirations of self-importance for the call that God had placed upon his life.

In our day, one man writes it this way: "High achievers nowa-days talk a lot about goal-setting. But they sometimes talk as if it doesn't really matter what goals we have as long as we have goals; targets to shoot at, dreams to pursue, any target, any dream. But not all goals are created equal."[5]

He goes on to say that good judgment is required when setting goals. Many people have been disappointed because, upon reaching their goals, found that nothing worthwhile was there. "True success," he continues, "is not just attaining goals. It is attaining goals that are worth attaining. . . . A beautiful house built on a bad foundation cannot provide for secure and stable long-term habitation."[6]

This conclusion reminds me of the wisdom Jesus shared when He said, "But everyone who hears these sayings of Mine, and does not do them, will be like a foolish man who built his house on the sand: and the rain descended, the floods came, and the winds blew and beat on that house; and it fell. And great was its fall" (Matthew 7:26–27). Good judgment comes from prayer, the goaltender of your goals. Prayer keeps you ever-dependent on the Lord as you trust Him and receive His direction.

So how can one be sure he or she is building on the right foundation? Perhaps the following re-summarization can help:

TIME management accomplishes GOALS
GOALS bring about PRIORITIES
PRIORITIES implement PHILOSOPHY
PHILOSOPHY guides PURPOSE
PURPOSE expresses IDENTITY
IDENTITY springs from THEOLOGY
All of these are based on the truth of God's Word!

When you make it your lifetime occupation to know who God is, you will progressively understand who you are in Him. As you are able to define your mission in life, you will make wise decisions that will be the guiding principles for direction. With these in place, you'll establish priorities that really matter and make wise commitments. This leads to confidence that those specific targets or marks will be pleasing and glorifying to the Lord.

Step Six: Celebration

A final and important part of the goal process is *celebration*. What runner does not celebrate a well-run race? In 1984, the women's marathon was introduced at the Summer Olympics in Los Angeles. Joan Benoit Samuelson overcame many barriers in order to compete in that event. In her high school, girls' track and field was not yet considered a varsity sport. But that did not discourage her from running. She persevered and eventually won the 1983 Boston Marathon as a college student at Bowdoin. But as the 1984 Games neared, Joan had to undergo arthroscopic knee surgery. Recovering more quickly than anyone anticipated, Joan won the Olympic trials seventeen days later. On August 5, Joan Benoit was in the lead in Los Angeles. Describing her feelings on that morning as she completed the final moments of her race, Joan said, "Coming into the Coliseum, I really didn't think anyone was going to be there. Who's going to come out and watch a bunch of women run in the first women's Olympic marathon on a Sunday morning? I really didn't think there would be a lot of people." Little did she know thousands were already on their feet ready to welcome the first winner of the women's Olympic marathon.[7] Celebration is the natural zenith of significant goal achievement.

God's people knew how to celebrate also. Look at the feasts, festivals, and worship services they held to commemorate their deliverance, the completion of their places of worship, and victories in battle over opponents.

It's good to remember to celebrate the goals God enables us to accomplish. These become specific, measurable marks that serve as reminders that we are truly living our theology, identity, purpose, philosophy, and priorities. They are visible milestones of God's faithfulness and grace. Even if it is a simple journal entry of thanksgiving or a few moments of spontaneous singing—celebrate! Have some friends over and tell them how God has helped you. Throw a party! Sanctify the moment!

Isn't it amazing what God has given us to carry out our God-given goals? Paul, in his letter to Timothy, encouraged the young man by reminding him of his calling, gifts, and opportunities. He reminded Timothy that the flame of potential needed to be fanned, not extinguished by a spirit of fear. Timothy had received power, love, and a sound mind. He was to build on that which God had given and carry on with the commitment. How often do we acknowledge and thank God for His power working in us?

Consider this story about one of the great mountains in the Alps. This mountain is popular with climbers because it has a rest stop about halfway up. If one starts at the base, the building can be reached at around lunch time.

Over the years, the owner of this rest stop has noticed an interesting phenomenon. When climbers get to this point, they feel the warmth of the fire, smell the good food, and begin to relax in the surroundings. Often, they will tell their companions to climb on without them. "We'll head back to base camp with you," they say, "on your way down."

A glazed look of contentment comes over them as they sit by the fire, play the piano, and sing mountain-climbing songs. In the meantime, the rest of the group get their gear and trek to the top. For the next couple of hours a spirit of happiness wafts through the house. "But," the owner says, "by midafternoon it starts to be quiet." The climbers who stayed behind begin taking turns looking out the window, staring at the top of the mountain. They're silent as they watch their friends reach the goal. The atmosphere changes from one of merriment to an almost funeral-like quietness as they realize that they forgot their commitment and settled for second-best. They missed the real celebration.[8]

The climbers who went on to reach the mountaintop not only *knew* they could do it, they *decided* they would do it. If God has put plans in your heart, then believe them to be possible. Build on the right foundation, bathe your goals in prayer, build toward them with the potential God has given you, and then believe it! Activate your faith by continuing on in your commitment, then remember to celebrate His faithfulness and grace when He finishes what He started.

It's Never Too Late

It's never too late to implement biblical, worthwhile goals through consecration, preparation, imagination, execution, evaluation, and celebration.

John Maxwell noted various individuals who discovered the value of new goals during their advanced years. Colonel Sanders, who originated "finger-licking-good" chicken, opened the first Kentucky Fried Chicken restaurant at age sixty-two. Casey Stengel, at seventy-five, was still managing the New York Mets baseball team. Picasso was still painting at eighty-eight. John Wesley still traveled on horseback to preach the gospel into his eighties.[9] All of these people had a vision. Their attitude, regardless of age, was to "press on."

What are you willing to commit yourself to regardless of age? How will you do it? When will you do it? Will it be because you know who God is? Because you know who you are in Him? And because you know why you are here, what you believe, and what really matters?

Henrietta Mears had big dreams for God. She discovered her passion for teaching Sunday school at the age of twelve. Using her gift of teaching, Mears made the Bible come alive for her students. Before she was forty, Henrietta had become the Director of Christian Education for the First Presbyterian Church in Hollywood, California. Over the next five years Sunday school attendance grew from 450 to over 6,000. Known for her unique sense of style and flamboyant hats, Henrietta's students simply referred to her as "Teacher." Henrietta understood what really mattered. Describing her commitment to teaching, she said, "When I consider my ministry, I think of the world. Anything less than that would not be worthy of Christ, or of his will for my life." Her vision of conquering the world for Christ influenced the vision of such notables as Billy Graham, Bill and Vonette Bright, and U.S. Senate Chaplain Richard Halverson.[10]

How will you do it? One day at a time, with solid consecration, thoughtful preparation, holy imagination, focused execution, careful evaluation, and joyful celebration. Commit to choose your marks not on whims, wishes, or wants but on the will and Word of God.

A Deeper Life Story

As a homeschooling mother of two, I have taught my daughters the importance of setting goals in order to achieve academic success. As parents, we wanted to teach our girls the importance of taking time to make a difference in the lives of others. Why not set goals for our family to do that?

The demands of raising a family can make it difficult to take the time to reach out to those in need of help, kindness, love, and most of all, a Savior. As I began evaluating the deep longings of my soul, I discovered that, as a family, we have demonstrated the priorities of using our time, talents, and treasures for the Lord. I felt that our girls were learning the importance of giving financially to our church, missions, and those in need. As a family, we have served in our church and community. While all of these are good things, there was still a desire to do more. That is when we decided to take the next step and set a goal for our first family missions trip.

By committing this desire to the Lord, we quickly learned through the process of consecration that His plan was different than ours. We desired to take the girls to Peru, but every door we attempted to pass through was quickly closed. The day after the last door closed on Peru, a new door opened for an opportunity to travel to Alaska. We knew this was related to the promise found in Proverbs 16:1: "The preparations of the heart belong to man, but the answer of the tongue is from the Lord."

We quickly began making preparations for a trip that was seven months away. I must admit that I was a bit unsure how God was going to provide the money that was necessary. My heart knew He was able, but my head couldn't wrap around what it would take to raise over $5,000. The entire family soon became involved in achieving our goal through working concession stands and holding a garage sale. At this writing, we only have a small amount left to reach our goal.

Imagining what this trip will be like for our family has carried us through the difficult steps of achieving this goal. We are focused daily on executing the plan and evaluating the progress. We look forward to the celebration this summer when we share the experience with our daughters, having developed a God-given goal in order to make a difference in the lives of others.

—Cheryl Morgan, mother and teacher

7

When Shall I Do It?

If I could, I would stand on a busy corner, hat in
hand, and beg people to throw me all their hours.
—*Bernard Berenson*

When I was a child I laughed and wept—
Time crept!
When as a youth I dreamed and talked—
Time walked!
When I became a full-grown man—
Time ran.
Then with the years I older grew—
Time flew!
Soon I shall find as I travel on—
Time gone!
—*Henry Twells*
(1823–1900)

A s I write this chapter, research tells us that nearly two-thirds of full-time workers own smartphones, up from 48 percent in just two years.[1] One-third own a tablet, up from 12 percent in the same two-year period. Like the incessant rush of water over Niagara Falls, it seems that our minds are always moving, our fingers are always typing, our lives are always interrupted, and our time is flowing away from us in unprecedented ways.

A front-page article of *USA Today* comments on our problem with time and technology: "Never clocking out has become so widespread that it has fueled a heated national debate on whether it is a benefit or detriment to society. . . . The exploding use of these devices—and connected employees never calling it a day—has created a workplace domino effect: If one person answers the boss's e-mail after hours, others feel compelled to as well." The article goes on to explain that people are tired of always being plugged in and that we have reached a tipping point where we are so overwhelmed and on edge from technology that we are craving a respite.

Millions of us work anywhere, anytime simply by pulling an iPhone or Android out of our purses or pockets. Two-thirds of U.S. employees now work during their vacations. Being constantly connected is taking a toll on our sleep, exercise time, and relationships.[2] With the apparent collapse of the space between work, leisure, and family, our concern about time management is greater than ever before.

Time and the Stewardship of Life

When it comes to getting a grip on time, it seems that the harder we work, the "behinder" we get. Physician and educator Richard Swenson wrote, "We talk of no time, the lack of time, not enough time, or being out of time, trying to get more time. We borrow time only to incur a time debt and end up with even less time." He observes that the atmosphere in the workplace is so time-management conscious that skills and time-compression techniques are constantly being sought. "This sense of time urgency," Swenson writes, "creates time pressure and time stress, and then it's crisis time."[3]

Ruthlessly eliminate hurry from your life

Time Defined

Just what is this thing called time? You can ask many different people and receive a variety of answers. A dictionary definition says that time is "a unit of geological chronology" or "any specified or defined period." I define time as my habitual expenditure of the stewardship of life.

Time is a "stewardship" because our lives are not our own. We tend to segment our understanding of time with labels like *work time, family time, leisure time, nap time, mealtime,* and the like. In reality, it is all *God's time.* Since it is His, we'd better be careful what we do with it.

Elisabeth Elliot expressed this same conviction when she said, "Time is a *creature*—a created thing—and a gift. We cannot make any more of it. We can only receive it and be faithful stewards in the use of it." [4] God has entrusted every person with life; time is life and life is time. Bottom line: Time speaks of the habits related to what I do with every twenty-four-hour segment that God grants me.

Some people have good habits when it comes to spending hours, minutes, and seconds. Others have developed unhealthy practices. Most of us have a few of each. But some people's habits turn into addictions.

Once curious about addictive habits, our preschool daughter wanted to know if an addiction was "kind of like what I have with my blankie?" She had been carrying her blanket around for a long time and confessed, "I said when I turned five I was going to give it up, but I keep asking for it every night. Is this an addiction?" Then our oldest son asked, "Is it kind of like baseball cards? The more I get, the more I want. Is this an addiction?"

Still, the greatest habit, and one that can be constructive or destructive, is the way we habitually spend our time. This is not an easy habit to change. It frustrates us because, again, the faster we go, the "behinder" we get.

Our History With Time

Frustration with time began early in man's history. A man named Plautus, in 200 BC, cursed a sundial. He uttered, "The gods confound the man who first found out how to distinguish hours . . . who in this place set up a sundial to cut and hack my day so wretchedly into small portions." [5]

Have you ever felt that way about time? Nearly fifty years ago futurists were peering into their crystal balls and predicting that one of the biggest problems for coming generations would be decisions concerning their abundance of spare time. Authorities testified before a Senate subcommittee in 1967 that by 1985 people could be working twenty-two hours a week or twenty-seven weeks a year, and could retire at age thirty-eight. Almost five decades have passed since then. Maybe I missed something.

"Paradoxical as it may seem," wrote economist E. F. Schumacher, "modern technological and industrial society, in spite of an incredible proliferation of labor-saving and time-saving devices, has not given people more time to devote to their all-important task of spiritual things. In fact, it has made it exceedingly difficult for anyone except the most determined to find any time whatever for these tasks." It is Schumacher's opinion that "the amount of genuine leisure available in a society is generally in inverse proportion to the amount of labor-saving technology it employs."[6] In a nutshell, the more sophisticated we become, the less time we have.

In the United States, time seems to be our master instead of our slave. In my travels to other countries, I find that time is handled differently. It seems to be associated more with relationships, the spiritual, the family, and the soul, than to a domineering wristwatch we wear. Whether I was in Indonesia, Romania, Nigeria, or Brazil, folks always seemed to have time for a leisurely cup of tea and a friendly chat.

Gandhi once said, "There is more to life than increasing its speed."[7] We can manage faster, write more rapidly, read more quickly, and communicate briefly. We have fast food, microwave meals, and ready-made snacks, and a world of information at our fingertips via the Internet. This tendency toward rushing occurs even within the walls of some churches that boast of offering eight- to twelve-minute sermons. This helps the listener to experience God faster?

Perhaps you have read the well-known piece of prose that says, "I have only just a minute, only sixty seconds in it, forced upon me, can't refuse it, but it's up to me to use it. I must suffer if I lose it, give account if I abuse it, just a tiny little minute, but eternity is in it." There's more to life than just increasing its speed.

The Practical Side of "The Time of Our Lives"

Given the exponential advance of sophistication in our society and our parallel struggle with limited time resources, the seminars and e-books on time management will likely be around beyond our lifetime. If we could only find time to attend those workshops and read the books, they might actually help us! I confess that over the years I have accumulated quite a collection of resources on time management. I've read dozens of books, listened to audio files, and attended the seminars. It does help to acquire tools for managing the minutes of your day. Appendix 13 offers "Quick Tips on Time Management" that might be helpful to you. However, the real key is to understand time from a biblical perspective.

The Biblical Perspective on Time

God's Word gives us a solid understanding of its concept of time. Paul wrote, "Be careful how you walk, not as unwise men but as wise, making the most of your time, because the days are evil. So then do not be foolish, but understand what the will of the Lord is" (Ephesians 5:15–17 NASB).

When Paul said to be careful how you walk, he was not referring to your choice of shoes, or watching where you put your feet. He was speaking about life, and the idea is to be careful. Foregoing a brief lesson in the Greek language, Paul's warning loosely translates this way: "Observe accurately, in a spirit of investigation, as you look at your life." (How you walk represents lifestyle and habits of behavior that result in the spending of your precious time) Paul cautions the reader to be wise, not foolish.

In Psalm 90:10–12, we see what wisdom looks like: "As for the days of our life, they contain seventy years, or if due to strength, eighty years, yet their pride is but labor and sorrow; for soon it is gone and we fly away. Who understands the power of Your anger, and Your fury, according to the fear that is due You? So teach us to number our days, that we may present to You a heart of wisdom" (NASB).

Paul also said to make "the most of your time, because the days are evil." He was not talking about modern time management, where the idea is to try to squeeze more seconds out of every minute. In Greek, the idea is purchasing something, or buying something back. Paul is saying, "Redeem the time." It's not yours automatically. You have to reach for it, seize it, and grasp it. Why? Because the days are evil.

The world's way of life will rob you. It's going to hold your time hostage unless you buy it back and take control of it, in the sense of using it for God's purposes, not evil. Someone or something is going to control your time expenditure. It will either be you or the world's beckoning call.

Chronos vs. Kairos

Let's pause for a moment to define two Greek words that translate into time. The first is *chronos*, from which we get the word *chronology*. This is the idea of continuous time that is measured in hours, minutes, or seconds—the clock that pushes us to the next appointment and runs out before we have finished with our daily responsibilities.

The second word for time is *kairos*, which is the idea of a fixed moment or season of opportunity. This is the period of the day when something special and truly memorable happens—a life experience when "time stands still."

Chronos is quantitative. *Kairos* is qualitative. The difference between these two words is the difference between a *minute* and a *moment*. A minute is measured by seconds, or by a clock. The experience and opportunity make up a moment.

The importance of moments versus minutes is seen in the way we treasure memories. When was the last time you heard someone say something like "Do you remember October 14, 2008? Wasn't that twenty-four-hour period truly life-changing?" Or have you ever said to anyone, "Do you remember that experience we shared at 3:17 p.m., two years ago?"

(We all recall with great fondness an event or relational encounter, not because of the date or time but because of the meaning of the moment. Days, hours, and minutes speak powerfully to our lives only when they have become the avenues of real "moments.") If we can understand, in retrospect, the value of moments versus minutes, wouldn't it be wise to do so with the present and future time that is before us!

minutes vs. moments

Truth Transcending Time

On November 19, 1863, a consecration service was held on a blood-covered battlefield at Gettysburg, Pennsylvania. Just that month 51,000 soldiers were killed, wounded, or missing in that decisive battle, so a national cemetery was being proposed for the site.

The original keynote speaker for this solemn ceremony was a man named Edward Everett. He was an extraordinary orator with cultured words, patriotic fervor, and public popularity. As a former governor and congressman, this sixty-nine-year-old statesman was a natural choice for this momentous gathering. Through an unanticipated turn of events, the commissioners of this service also invited President Abraham Lincoln. When the commissioners learned that the president planned to attend, they asked him to offer "a few appropriate remarks" as well.

When the day came, Everett rose to give his speech according to plan. His memorized oratory flowed with masterful fluctuation and dramatic gestures. Everyone, including President Lincoln, was captured by his eloquence. Finally, an hour and fifty-seven minutes later, Everett concluded, and the crowd applauded enthusiastically.

A short time afterward, President Lincoln stepped to the podium. His notes consisted of two simple handwritten pages, with thoughts born out of his own great burden and tears over the wartime situation of the country he led and loved. With very little gesturing, but deep personal passion, he delivered his own Gettysburg Address. In two minutes he was finished.[8]

Almost one hundred and forty years have passed since that day of solemn remembrance. No one can recall one line from the two-hour speech of the orator. Yet Lincoln's two minutes of passion—flowing from deep conviction and clear purpose—are among the most memorable thoughts in the history of our nation. This illustrates the difference between minutes and moments.

Seizing the Moments

Paul did not use *chronos* when he said to make the most of your time. The idea isn't to control your hours and minutes or to fill in your daily and weekly schedules. He was not talking about any time-management system. He was talking about buying back the moments, not the minutes.

We are dealing with *kairos*, the opportunities God brings across our paths. Paul, in effect, was saying, "You've got to aggressively buy this time back or you're going to miss the God-given moment." Capture the moments, seize them, and buy them back from a world that is stealing them away!

Think of the people in Noah's day who missed that pivotal moment in time. Generations later, another moment was missed when Jesus entered Jerusalem and walked among the people. They failed to grasp the important opportunity. How did Jesus respond? He wept. (See Luke 19:28–44.)

Biblical Time Management

Biblical time management is not so much a matter of controlling the calendar but of capitalizing on opportunities. Any number of books and seminars can teach you the fine art of making lists, ordering tasks, handling interruptions, dealing with paperwork, and staying on top of emails. This chapter is about understanding, anticipating, and maximizing the "moments" of your life—an often overlooked and ultimately important issue of time management.

An ancient Greek statue depicts a man with wings on his feet, a large lock of hair on the front of his head, and no hair on the back of his head. Beneath this statue is the following inscription:

> Who made thee? Lucipius made me.
> What is thy name? My name is opportunity.
> Why hast thou wings on thy feet?
> That I may fly away swiftly.
> Why hast thou a great forelock?
> That men may seize me when I come.
> Why art thou bald in back? That when I am
> gone none can lay hold of me.[9]

This is what Paul meant. Opportunity has wings on its feet, and it must be seized in advance, as it comes, as it is here. Once gone, the possibility of grasping it is gone. Control your time from this biblical time-management wisdom. Instead of mastering your calendar, become a master of your opportunities.

Time-management wisdom is summed up in these words: "Do not be foolish, but understand what the will of the Lord is" (Ephesians 5:17 NASB). And how does one understand? Let me restate the obvious but essential principle: Understanding the "will of the Lord" as it pertains to time is to face our days based on the foundation of theology, identity, purpose, values, priorities, and goals.

This means walking in dependence upon Him, being filled with the Spirit of God. The Spirit gives us understanding, wisdom, and insight into the truth of God. This enables us to see the opportunities, seize the time, and become wise stewards of the habits of our daily lives.

practical app. of opportunity

Jesus is the supreme example of how to properly use time. He lived with a perfect heart of understanding. He said that He came "not to do My own will, but the will of Him who sent Me" (John 6:38). Along with this understanding was a sense of urgency. In John 9:4, we read Jesus' words: "We must work the works of Him who sent Me as long as it is day; night is coming when no one can work" (NASB). The foundation of understanding time is seen in the importance and needfulness of doing God's will.

Christ's Firm Grasp of Opportunity

As we continue to learn from Jesus' example, we see Him ministering with a firm grasp on opportunity. In John 7, all Jews were going to Jerusalem to celebrate the Feast of the Tabernacles. Jesus saw this opportunity, not from the standpoint of when the Feast began (*chronos*), but from the understanding that this was the time to accomplish God's purpose (*kairos*). Members of His family were pushing Him to immediately go and prove himself publicly, but He replied, "Go up to the feast yourselves; I do not go up to this feast because My time has not yet fully come" (v. 8 NASB). *Chronos* time may have come for the Feast, but the *kairos* opportunity was not yet there. God-given opportunity does not always happen according to a clock but according to the moment of eternal significance.

Even in the hour of His crucifixion, Jesus was obediently aware of the passing moments. "For this purpose I came to this hour," He said (John 12:27). Later we read, "Jesus knew that His hour had come that He should depart out of this world to the Father" (13:1). This is our example of wise time management, a pattern to follow when making habitual decisions.

Christ's Perfect Display of Wisdom

When it came to His limited time on earth, Jesus showed perfect wisdom. This was particularly true in two areas: renewal and reproduction. In Matthew 14, Jesus received some very heavy and troubling news. His dear cousin and forerunner, John, had just been beheaded: "When Jesus heard it, He departed from there by boat to a deserted place by Himself" (v. 13). The multitude followed Him, though, and without any sign of resentment or stress, He fed thousands with five loaves and two fish. After the masses had left, He returned again to His priority need to go away "by Himself to pray" (v. 23). This was a regular part of his habitual expenditure of the stewardship of life (as confirmed in Mark 1:35 and Luke 22:39). What wisdom for those who wish to find a pattern for the wise use of time.

Jesus also knew the wisdom of habitually investing His tim
reproducing His character and life in those who would carry the
torch to the next generation. As He drew closer to the time of His
death, He spent increasing amounts of time with His inner team
of disciples. The fruit of this investment was seen as He prayed
in the garden to His Father just before He was to die. He said, "I
have glorified You on the earth. I have finished the work which
You have given Me to do. . . . I have manifested Your name to the
men whom You have given Me out of the world. They were Yours,
You gave them to Me, and they have kept Your word" (John 17:4,
6). Jesus truly is the perfect model of what it means to redeem the
time wisely.

Finding *Kairos* in the Chaos of *Chronos*

Most of our time planning has to do with the minutes of life rather
than the moments that count. However, biblical emphasis is almost
the opposite. This does not mean we should neglect structure and
organization. After all, "God is not the author of confusion" (1 Corinthians 14:33). What it does show is that we have not understood
the value of time until we firmly grasp, actively anticipate, and
purposefully pursue the moments God places before us. We can
learn to seize the moments, not just spend the minutes.

As to finding *kairos* in the chaos of our *chronos*, we must first
realize that moments can indeed be found in the midst of our
chaotic schedules. And they are chaotic. It is said that the average
office worker in America is interrupted seven times an hour,[10] with
office distractions eating up 2.1 hours a day.[11] No wonder. We now
receive as many as 5,000 advertising messages in a day.[12] Our time
spent on social media in 2012 in this country totaled 121 billion
minutes.[13] Time management experts now consider Twitter as the
silent productivity killer.[14] We spend so much time on our electronic
devices that half of office workers polled admitted to answering
emails in bed.[15]

With such a pace, it's comforting to know that while moments
and minutes are distinctive and may often have to be handled   139

separately, in the course of a day we can choose to make a moment out of any minute and buy back the time.

Eternal Moments With Your Eternal God

Speaking of decisions, wise time management includes the decision to capture moments for personal renewal. All of this talk about making wise choices, changing bad habits for good ones, and incorporating truth into lifestyle can be overwhelming at the outset. As we've already seen, Jesus understood the necessity of spending time in the Father's presence. His habit was to rise early and to find a solitary place in which to pray. Because of this practice, He was enabled to minister effectively when the opportunities arose.

Many of us are impatient with the things of God because we don't take time for God. We fail to buy back, or redeem, these precious moments. Consequently, we fail to minister in His wisdom, will, and Spirit. We lose opportunities and don't use time to its full advantage. Time for daily renewal brings us into the *kairos* mode so we can see the moments of life more clearly.

The Living Bible paraphrases Proverbs 10:27 in this manner: "Reverence for God adds hours to each day." Jill Briscoe sheds light on this priority when she writes, "No one has any more time than you have. It is the discipline and stewardship of your time that is important. The management of time is the management of self; therefore, if you manage time with God, He will begin to manage you."[16]

Significant periods of renewal and reflection are perhaps one of the most powerful tools for true biblical time management. Jesus knew the value of time alone in the wilderness. The early church pursued extended days of prayer. Biblical examples show us that many of the great personalities sought extensive amounts of time for renewal. They knew they must "come apart" before they "came apart."

This is vital to true integrity. If you are to integrate your time usage with your theology, then it is vital to spend time with the God of your theological foundation. He is also the God of your new man, your purposes, values, priorities, and goals. Maintaining and cherishing spiritual renewal will make all the difference.

Eternal Moments for Eternal Souls

One of the most important elements in *kairos* living is remembering to be open to the people who enter into your daily life. Are you ready and willing to make an eternal impact on them, or is your day so tightly scheduled that God-given purpose is forgotten? Wise time management includes being open to the spontaneous work of the Holy Spirit.

Every seemingly mundane minute, when spent with another person, carries the potential of a *kairos* moment. It's been said, "Time, wisely used, gives relationships top priority." A lunch appointment can be a moment of sharing the good news of Jesus Christ with the server. The usual meeting at work can close with a moment of impact as you speak a caring word or a genuine compliment. The Bible tells us, "Conduct yourselves with wisdom toward outsiders, making the most of the opportunity. Let your speech always be with grace, as though seasoned with salt, so that you may know how you should respond to each person" (Colossians 4:5–6 NASB).

Instead of simply taking your children to the grocery store, plan to talk on the way about principles that matter. On the return trip, stop for ice cream. Between licks, remind them of how important they are to you and why. This turns a menial trip into a meaningful moment.

Another way of making the most of your time, from an eternal perspective, is to learn how to bring the presence of God, and your dependence on Him, into the minutes of your day. When driving, instead of listening to the radio, spend your trip-time praying. Pray about your life. Pray for open doors of ministry. Pray for your family. Pray for the people in the cars around you and see the masses as Jesus sees them, with compassion rather than frustration. This is called "praying on site, with insight." It can be done anywhere and at any time. Necessary errands become encounters with eternity and minutes turn into moments.

While modern time-management tools tell us how to get more done with our minutes, God's wisdom (seeing life from an eternal perspective) tells us how to get more life into our moments. As Proverbs 9:11 affirms, "I, Wisdom, will make the hours of your day more profitable and the years of your life more fruitful" (TLB).

Numbering Our Fleeting Days

I'll never forget a story that spoke to my heart about the limited amount of time we have left here on earth. Del Fehsenfeld Jr., founder of a ministry called Life Action, wrote about a family friend who had recently died as a result of a motorcycle accident.

> From a human vantage point, there were a number of reasons why those who knew David and loved him were shocked by the news of his death. David was a strong, healthy twenty-two-year-old college student. He was generous, big-hearted, and had a seemingly infinite capacity to love people. He was in school preparing for a lifetime of ministry. The possibilities of this dedicated young man's future seemed limitless. So it was natural to feel that the "timer" on David's life had run out too soon. Yet we know that the timer on each of our lives is held and controlled by the righteous, wise hand of our loving heavenly Father. . . .
>
> It is so easy to presume upon the future. "Tomorrow I'll get serious about spiritual growth . . ." "When I finish this project, I'll start spending more time with my wife and kids . . ." "One of these days I'll make restitution for that item I stole . . ." "Someday I'll seek forgiveness from the parent I rebelled against . . ." And on and on we go, living in the world of tomorrow. The only problem is, tomorrow may never come. . . .
>
> According to Psalm 90, God grants us about seventy years on the average. Seventy years—just 25,550 days. I have already spent over 14,000 of those days. If God is gracious, I may have another 11,000 days or so in which to glorify and please Him.
>
> But there is no guarantee that I will be given many days. God gave my friend David only 8,267 days. God gave His only Son 12,000 days in which to accomplish His plan on this earth. However, as the moment approached when the "timer" on His life

would be finished, Jesus was able to say, "I have glorified thee on the earth: I have finished the work which thou gavest me to do" (John 17:4 KJV).

For every one of us, at the end of our days there will come a time when we must give an account of how we invested those days. Unfortunately, when God calls "Time's up!" many of us will be caught off-guard. We may want to protest, "But I was just getting started!" Then with shame we will have to confess that our days were spent pursuing our own pleasure and goals, and that while we gave lip service to the lordship of Jesus Christ, in reality, we lived for ourselves . . . .

So, Lord, teach us to number our days.[17]

Just 852 days after this article was published, Del learned he was dying of brain cancer. Two hundred and thirty-five days after that, he stepped into eternity, leaving his wife and family of five children. In the article he talked about maybe having 11,000 more days in addition to the 14,000 he'd already spent. Instead, he lived only slightly more than 1,000 days.

That, my friend, is why the issue of "When shall I do it?" is one of the eight most important questions you will ever ask. The time to ask is today, not tomorrow, or next week. If God has touched your heart, seize the moment now. Begin a biblical, habitual expenditure of the stewardship of life through strategic daily renewal and "win" the battle for time.

> He was going to be all that a mortal could be . . .
> No one should be kind nor braver than he . . .
> Tomorrow;
>
> A friend who was troubled and weary he knew
> Who'd be glad for a lift and who needed it, too;
> On him would he call and see what he could do . . .
> Tomorrow.
>
> Each morning he stacked up the letters he'd write . . .
> And thought of the folks he would fill with delight . . .
> Tomorrow;

143

It was too bad, indeed, he was busy today,
And hadn't a minute to stop on his way;
"More time I'll have to give others," he'd say . . .
"Tomorrow."

The greatest of workers this man would have been . . .
The world would have known him had he ever seen . . .
Tomorrow;

But the fact is he died, and he faded from view,
And all that he left here when living was through
Was a mountain of things he intended to do . . .
Tomorrow.

Attributed to Edgar Guest

A Deeper Life Story

A wise friend once told me that time is more valuable than money. As a young stay-at-home mom, I embraced that concept and became determined to manage the time I had with my children while they were still in my care. Two weeks ago, we celebrated the wedding of our daughter—our last child to be married. It was a precious moment in time. A **kairos** moment.

I first learned of the concept of **kairos** vs. **chronos** several years ago when Daniel Henderson taught in the Sunday school class I was attending. He described how "every seemingly mundane minute, when spent with another person, carries the potential of a **kairos** moment of eternally significant impact."

When I think of a life lived with a **kairos** mentality, I think of my friend Dr. Jill Jones, the most intentional person I have ever met. With her, there were no wasted minutes, no trivial conversations. If you sat across the table from Jill, she asked about your life—your hopes, dreams, fears, or spiritual growth. As a professor at a Christian university, she became involved in the lives of hundreds of students. She demonstrated her burden for them by beginning each class on her knees in prayer.

In the midst of her busy schedule of teaching and raising two teenage sons, Jill carved out time to write a book. **The Princess**

Journal told of Jill's personal journey, a story she felt compelled to share with the world and especially with her family. Shortly after the book's publication, Jill's sister read the book and received Christ as her Savior. A few months later, Jill and her sixteen-year-old son were killed by a drunk driver.

In the days following her death, I stopped into Jill's office to gather a few of her belongings for her family. Although her summer had been spent teaching several intensive classes, it struck me that Jill's desk was clean. No piles of papers or textbooks—only a single handwritten note that read: "Nehemiah 6:15—the completion of the wall." Jill had been studying the book of Nehemiah, learning how to build with one hand while keeping a sword in the other. The verse speaks of the wall being built in fifty-two days, quite an accomplishment. Although Jill's time on earth was brief, forty-two short years, only God knows what she was able to accomplish with the moments He gave her.

Even her final minutes on earth were spent with purpose, expressing love for the man who would soon feel the unimaginable loss of his wife and son. In the moments before the crash, as her son, Niko, drove them home from a long trip, Jill posted a final message to her Facebook wall: "Home . . . It truly is where your heart (husband) is!!!" And on August 8, 2010, Jill's wall was completed.

—Brenda Brown, women's ministry leader

8

How Will I Finish?

The great use of one's life is to spend it on something that will outlast it. For the value of life is computed, not by its duration but by its donation.

—*William James*

An inheritance is what we leave for others. A legacy is what we leave in them.

—*Source unknown*

When you woke up this morning, it is possible you started your day believing a lie. The deception is subtle, even subconscious, and it is seldom articulated or analyzed. What is this lie? *It does not matter how you live your life, why you live your life, or even that you live your life.*

But the truth is, the world around you *needs* your legacy. The drama, defeats, determination, and dialogue of your journey offer meaning to eager hearts—around the world and right under your nose.

Today, the world you step into looks like this:

- 1.75 billion people are desperately poor.[1]
- One billion are hungry.[2]

- Each year nearly two million children are exploited in the global commercial sex trade, the second largest organized crime in the world.[3]
- Before you finish reading the next few pages, almost ninety children will die of preventable diseases.[4]

This morning, if you live in the United States, you'll exist in a society that shows evidence of moral and spiritual implosion:

- Only 17 percent attend church on any given Sunday.[5]
- Approximately 2.6 million people leave the church every decade.[6]
- Those claiming no religion in the U.S. have almost doubled in the last decade.[7]
- Evangelicals now account for only 10 percent of the population.
- Approximately 1,500 pastors a month leave the ministry in the United States.[8]

More important, as you make your morning coffee, glance at the family pictures on the walls of your home, and check your Facebook updates by friends and associates, you should realize:

- Your spouse needs you to be a spiritual anchor in a world gone adrift.
- Your children or grandchildren are crying out for an example of how to live their lives with integrity.
- Every one of your friends is hungry for an encouraging word from someone who understands the meaning of this earthly journey.
- Your work and ministry associates need a model that stands out and stands apart from the confusing blueprint of our out-of-control world.

The circulating lie is that only a select and special minority make a significant impact on this world. But if legacy were primarily about money, only the rich would matter. If legacy were about

achievement, only the driven and extraordinarily skilled would count. If legacy were about knowledge, only those with superior IQs would be respected.

The truth is, everyone has the potential for leaving a legacy in this life. This chapter will help you understand why—and how.

Legacy: The Crowning Memoir of a Deeper Life

In 2012, The Script, an Irish rock band, released the song "Hall of Fame." Hugely popular, the music video pictured an aspiring young boxer alongside a hopeful ballerina, both with serious disadvantages but big dreams. The lyrics describe the potential of any person—preacher, teacher, or politician to achieve their own "hall of fame." Agree with the lyrics or not, the song resonated powerfully in the souls of a young generation that longs to leave a legacy. Every generation knows this yearning.

Charles Dickens wrote, "Come out into the world about you, be it either wide or limited. Sympathize, not in thought only, but in action, with all about you. Make yourself known and felt for someone that would be loved and missed, in twenty thousand little ways, if you were to die; then your life will be a happy one, believe me."

Mike Pfau, a friend and accomplished life coach, said it this way: "Something I've noticed over and over in my work is this: The longing of every heart is 'Did I matter? Does my life make a difference?' Some are even so bold as to ask, 'How will the world be different because I was here?'" Let's be bold—and human— and honest. We want the world to be different because we were part of it.

Legacy is defined as something transmitted by or received from another who has preceded us in this life. But this simple description hardly captures the essence of this eighth and ultimately important question.

In the end, a deeper life must be a life deposited into the fertile soil of eternal souls through the transforming seeds of truth. Integrity is a priority for every life. Integrity invested in others is priceless in every generation. A legacy is an eternally significant investment of one's life in the lives of others. Legacy allows each 149 of us to "outlive our life" and leave behind a testimony of worship, integrity, and nonconformity in this world.

I hope by now you have been deeply challenged to live with a rock-solid, regularly reaffirmed foundation of knowing God, embracing your core identity, and affirming God's purpose for your life. I pray that your desire to live by a clear set of values—embracing the best priorities and fulfilling those priorities through meaningful goals and effective use of time—is being fulfilled. Yet the end game of this process of daily renewal is that you leave a legacy for others to embrace and experience for their own good. As you make time to clarify your answers to the foundational questions of this book, you are not just penning words or typing ideas, you are crafting an autobiography to be read by those walking in your footsteps.

Benjamin Franklin said, "If you would not be forgotten as soon as you are dead, either write something worth reading or do something worth writing." This book, and your engagement with the process of strategic daily renewal, is intended to help you compose the insurance policy of an unforgettable life.

We've heard many times that it's not how you start the race but how you finish that matters. Legacy really is at the core of asking, "How will I finish?" We cannot control when we will hit the finish line of life, but we can intentionally focus our energies on how we will cross that line.

Eternal Significance, Not Earthly Success

When I begin to evaluate the significance of my life by the super-achievers on the covers of magazines, the vacations my friends have taken that I cannot afford, or the plethora of other superficial markers of a "meaningful" life, I tell myself, *The scoreboard is in heaven.* (I actually have to remind myself often.)

In this life, every temporal contest has a visible scoreboard. Some are on Jumbotrons at the pinnacle of a massive coliseum. Others are parked in the home garage. Some flash on the ticker at Wall Street. Winning in this life is quantified by touchdowns, home runs, industrial averages, the square footage of a walk-in closet, or the degrees behind a name. Of course, ambition, accumulation, and achievement are not necessarily wrong. But the motivation behind them can be very slippery. It can all become very one-dimensional—the temporal dimension.

Paul acknowledged this when he wrote, "Do you not know that those who run in a race all run, but one receives the prize?" (1 Corinthians 9:24). Then, speaking of the world's short-lived rat race, Paul observes, "They do it to obtain a perishable crown" (v. 25). Translation: Their motive and measure is temporal.

I'll never forget hearing the story of a successful Christian businessman who worked from an opulent penthouse office of a downtown high-rise. On his desk he kept a plaque that helped him keep perspective: "It's all going to burn." He was right. God had granted him earthly success, but he did not want to forget eternal significance.

Paul taught that everything we do as believers will someday be revealed "by fire" in a final test of the eternal value of our earthly appearance (1 Corinthians 3:12–15). This fire of divine scrutiny will determine the "sort" of life we lived—not the scope, size, or sizzle. Eugene Peterson, in *The Message*, paraphrases this passage: "Take particular care in picking out your building materials. Eventually there is going to be an inspection. If you use cheap or inferior materials, you'll be found out. The inspection will be thorough and rigorous. You won't get by with a thing."

The good news for legacy-leavers is that we can build our lives with "gold, silver, precious stones"—eternal and enduring aspirations that are about worship, integrity, and nonconformity. Returning to Paul's description of life's contest, we can run the race of this life to win "an imperishable crown." This requires spiritual discipline and an unselfish focus (1 Corinthians 9:24–27).

What You Pass On, Not What You Possess

Andrew Carnegie, one of the wealthiest U.S. businessmen of the nineteenth century, summarized it well: "No man becomes rich unless he enriches others."

J. Paul Getty is still remembered today as one of the richest men in American history. After graduating from Oxford University in 1913, Getty followed his father's footsteps into the oil business. By age twenty-three, he was a millionaire. Getty was recognized by *Fortune Magazine* in 1957 as the richest man in the world, with a net worth of billions.

In spite of his impressive financial ledger, his legacy faltered. Getty's success was only outpaced by his stinginess.[9] He was rarely generous with his fortunes or his life. For example, at his sixteenth-century English manor, Sutton Place, located on 700 acres outside London, Getty installed a pay phone so his guests would not take advantage of him by making personal calls on his nickel.

In 1973, his sixteen-year-old grandson was kidnapped in Italy and held for a ransom of $17 million. Getty refused to part with his money for the freedom of his grandson. Not until the boy's right ear was cut off by his captors and mailed to a Rome newspaper did Getty give serious consideration to complying with their demands. Even then, he claimed he could only raise $2.7 of $17 million. After five long months of captivity and trauma, the boy was eventually found alive near Naples.[10]

When Getty died in 1976, he left behind an alienated family, five ex-wives fighting one another in court for his 4-billion-dollar fortune, and a reputation of miserliness. Most of Getty's fortune went to his namesake museum in Los Angeles.

In contrast, his son J. Paul Getty Jr., gave millions of dollars away from his reduced portion of the inheritance. He commented, "I regard myself as a custodian of that money for the benefit of people who need it more than I do."[11]

Legacy is not about what you gain from this life but what you give. Even people of meager means and difficult circumstances can focus their life on a greater cause and the needs of others.

- Moses refused a life of privilege to wander in the desert with a tribe of countless rebellious people—but God gave him the privilege of communicating the Ten Commandments, foundational truth that has shaped entire societies.

- For many years of his life Joseph had no family, no home, no rights, and no hope—but he left a legacy of wisdom and provision for an entire nation, including his family.
- The boy with a simple lunch had only two fish and five small loaves—but he left a legacy of miraculous provision through his availability and surrender.
- The early disciples were men of simple, even disregarded, professions—but they left the legacy of a transformed world.
- Timothy was young and timid—but the great apostle Paul trusted him to carry on his legacy, and many are believers today because of their faithfulness.

How Well You Lived, Not How Long

I've always been impressed with distance runners who know how to excel in a race of multiple laps or even many miles. A key to their performance in long-distance competition is the ability to "kick" in a burst of energy in the final segment of the contest. Usually the winner's best effort is his last one, as he engages a sprint-like reserve to finish the race at a profound pace.

Knowing the Christian life is a long-distance event compels us to ask the questions: How will I end the race? What will my spiritual pace look like as I approach the finish line? Will my last lap be my best one? Or will I dribble across the finish line with a "spiritual retirement" mindset, running without purpose?

Paul finished impressively. In what amounted to the final press of his pen to the parchment, he wrote,

> For I am already being poured out as a drink offering, and the time of my departure is at hand. I have fought the good fight, I have finished the race, I have kept the faith. Finally, there is laid up for me the crown of righteousness, which the Lord, the righteous Judge, will give to me on that Day, and not to me only but also to all who have loved His appearing.
>
> 2 Timothy 4:6–8

Paul was so spiritually resolute in his final steps before touching eternity's tape that he described his death as an act of worship. He spoke with passion about the grace of God that enabled him to finish his race and spoke with great anticipation of the crown that made every effort worth it. We do not know exactly how many years Paul lived, and really it does not matter because this life is a "vapor," whether it is eight years, eighteen years, or eighty-one years. We do know how intentionally Paul lived. His legacy tells the story.

I'll never forget Chet, a man who attended a three-day men's prayer summit that I led in Minnesota. He was ninety-eight years old. Not only was I astonished that he was willing to commit to this very intense, unscripted, multi-day prayer experience—but I was even more amazed with his active participation during the entire event. He watched, he listened, he sang, and he prayed with an open heart and joyful attitude.

On the final evening of the summit, we enjoyed a two-hour Communion experience. The service included the option for the men to wash the feet of the others at a prayer station in the back of the room, if they felt led to do so. Of course, a handful of younger men were eager to honor Chet by washing his feet. One of our leaders, observing it all, said that Chet also washed the feet of some of the men. The entire time Chet did this, he quoted an array of Scripture passages from memory.

Billy Graham wrote, "No matter who we are, retirement presents us with two choices. Either we can use it to indulge ourselves, or we can use it to make an impact on the lives of others. In other words, the choice we face is between empty self-indulgence and meaningful activity. Will we seek God's plan for our retirement years? Or will we drift aimlessly along, assuming our usefulness is over and spend the rest of our days trying to squeeze as much enjoyment as we can out of life?"[12]

But many of us will not live as long as Chet, or Billy Graham, or even the average person. Some never reach retirement age. What about their legacy?

David Brainerd was a missionary to the American Indians in New York, New Jersey, and eastern Pennsylvania. Born in Connecticut in 1718, he died of tuberculosis at the age of twenty-nine. One biographer summarizes Brainerd's punctuated life in these words:

> His *Diary* and *Journal* are abrim with ministries and miracles that were akin to the Acts of the Apostles. The *Life and Diary of David Brainerd* ought to be read—and read often—by God's people. It will do something for you spiritually. You will be convicted, challenged, changed, [and] charged. It has had life-transforming effect upon many, motivating them to become missionaries, evangelists, preachers, people of prayer and power with God. Brainerd's centuries-spanning influence for revival is positive proof God can and will use any vessel, no matter how fragile and frail, if it is only sold out to souls and the Savior![13]

Over my years of pastoral ministry, I've conducted scores of funeral and memorial services. Many of these celebrated a life well-lived for Christ, and others . . . not so much. Yet the ones that stand out as having a profound impact on others were in connection with a child or teenager. In each case, the auditorium was packed with young people, families, and many who would have never otherwise even been in a church building. If the purpose of any life, short or long, is the proclamation of the gospel, then these punctuated lives were well-lived. Ironically, in their premature death, they had more kingdom impact than many who live for decades without any particular contribution to the lives of others.

Over the years I've said, "It's not how long you've been in the boat, it is how effectively you've been paddling." Years of age are not necessarily the same as depth of influence. Chronological maturity and effective ministry are not always mutually inclusive.

Faith Zone, Not Comfort Zone

I reflect often that the comfort zone is the danger zone. When we play it safe in life and avoid risky obedience, we dilute the impact of our legacy. Hebrews 11:6 reminds us, "Without faith it is impossible to please God." The comfort zone requires little faith. Rather, we meander in the gray twilight of predictability, ease, and commonplace influence.

Hebrews 11 is the chapter that describes faith and then illustrates it in the lives of common people who lived with an uncommon obedience. They followed unpredictable paths, left security, and in some cases paid with their lives. Their legacy lives on in the pages of the Bible.

Steve Saint, renowned for his book and the subsequent film *End of the Spear*, understood risk. His father, Nate Saint, was a missionary pilot who was killed while seeking to reach the Wadoni tribe (then known as the Auca Indians) in Ecuador in 1956. Steve's life continued the legacy of sacrifice and missionary enterprise as he has risked much, often returning to Ecuador over the years to minister to the people who took his father's life. As Steve noted, "Your story is the greatest legacy that you will leave to your friends. It's the longest-lasting legacy you will leave to your heirs."

Jim Elliot, also among those killed by the Aucas in 1956, is remembered for his famous line, written in a journal some years before his death: "He is no fool who gives what he cannot keep to gain that which he cannot lose." The toys and attractions of the comfort zone will someday be gone and forgotten. A life given for noble purposes will leave a branding of inspiration in the hearts of many.

Passed on Through People, Not Productivity

I have a task-oriented, results-focused personality. This has served me well in driving me toward achievement, but I fear it has undermined my legacy. At the end of our lives, our projects will be forgotten. Our awards will be discarded. Our degrees will be meaningless. Our legacy will instead be told through people.

I've always been amazed that the final discharge on the scroll from the ink of the apostle Paul's pen, as he wrote from a dank and dirty prison to his devoted disciple Timothy, was largely given to his commentary about people. I would expect him to unpack some final glorious theological treatise. Instead, he talks about the people he's worked with, the ones who have hurt and disappointed him, and the friends he wanted to acknowledge through personal greetings. After all his experience and exploits, his final thoughts were about people.

In the previous chapter, we looked at the use of our time and how it should be focused on the value of eternal souls. We must remember, when our time has ended, those eternal souls will carry forward the memory and meaning of our lives long after we are gone.

John Maxwell has noted, "Success is when the people who know you best respect you the most." A reputation of accomplishment can often be a house of cards. Real success is the legacy we have deposited in the hearts of those closest to us in this life.

Intentionality, Not Infallibility

Only imperfect people leave a legacy. A legacy is not about some standard of unachievable virtue. Legacies are not made of super-sanitized stories and better-than-thou behaviors. Rather, the inspiration of a legacy is composed of difficulties endured, mistakes made right, lessons learned through pain, and tough relationships graced by the power of forgiveness and reconciliation.

I remember a wise, highly accomplished businessman giving me some advice when I was just twenty-eight. I had been thrust into a role of responsibility far beyond my experience. With conviction and clarity, he told me, "The most important decision is the second decision." He elaborated on the uncompromising commitment to evaluate every choice and make it better when necessary. He spoke of the humility of recognizing a mistake and making it right—thoroughly and immediately. He spoke of the conviction to recognize offensive words or actions and to decisively make things right and move on with an unencumbered soul and clear conscience. A legacy is all about "second decisions."

I often say that God's only inventory is "cracked pots." Eugene Peterson captured it this way, "We carry this precious Message around in the unadorned clay pots of our ordinary lives. That's to prevent anyone from confusing God's incomparable power with us" (2 Corinthians 4:7 MESSAGE). The raw material of an imperfect   157 life is the mud in the Master Potter's hands that becomes a life remembered. When the clay remains pliable through transparency, authenticity, unselfishness, and grace, the masterpiece of worship, integrity, and nonconformity emerges to the glory of God and the good of others.

Commit to the WIN of a Deeper Life

I hope you feel empowered with the assurance that you can truly live a life of lasting influence. Now, what can you do every day—for many days—to eventually shape a legacy that will be remembered long after you are gone? Consider these practical reminders.

The hard part about leaving a legacy is that it can only be fashioned over time and in the whirlwind of relentless spiritual battle. That's the nature of life. Because it is hard to navigate in a vortex, the daily commitment to this entire renewal process is vital.

I remember consulting with one of my mentors during a very difficult season of ministry. He listened and then also shared some stories from a chapter of his own life, one that was also painful. He offered practical wisdom I will never forget: "I decided that I could not waste my energies on things I could not control. I had to give my best efforts every day to what I COULD control." He could not control the attitudes of other people, the reaction of his critics, or the attendance figures of the church. He *could* control his own walk with God, his attitude, his exercise and diet routines, and his primary relationships.

Each of us must give relentless attention to the daily issues we can control. That is why our worship, integrity, and nonconformity to the world are vital for building a legacy—one day at a time.

Commit to a Christ-Centered Lifestyle

Jesus did not tell us to "figure it out." He simply said, "Follow me." As we follow Jesus, we are compelled to live untethered from the world's definitions of success. When our impact is forged by walking in the ways of the Savior, it will cost us. The price will be felt in our surrender to God and our sacrifice for others. As one friend says, "It does cost to follow Jesus Christ. But it costs even more not to follow Him." One of the things not following will cost us is a legacy.

Commit to Living in the Spirit

The supernatural power of the indwelling Spirit shapes our character, empowers our testimony, imparts supernatural endurance, and builds our legacy in others. Spirit-imparted authenticity attracts people. Acts 4:13 tells us the "untrained and uneducated" disciples of Jesus caused the religious leaders of the day to "marvel." Their amazement was spurred by the spiritual boldness that emanated from Peter and John, which was the obvious overflow of their intimacy with Jesus, by the power of the Holy Spirit. Second Corinthians 4:2 explains our impact with these words, "By manifestation of the truth [we are] commending ourselves to every man's conscience in the sight of God."

Real legacies do not point to the unachievable exploits of a bigger-than-life personality. They do not intimidate people with superiority. Rather they draw others into a deeper spirituality, which is available to anyone who possesses the all-sufficient Spirit of God. Paul spoke transparently of this when describing his desire to influence others. He explained to his followers that the elements of his ministry "were not with persuasive words of human wisdom, but in demonstration of the Spirit and of power, that your faith should not be in the wisdom of men but in the power of God" (1 Corinthians 2:4–6).

Commit to Tangible Testimonials

Just as God provided His people with tangible testimonials of His work, we are wise to consider practical things to pass down, pointing to the real meaning of our life. Beyond heirlooms or keepsakes, we can leave memorials to inspire those who follow us in this life.

When the children of Israel were delivered from slavery in Egypt, the Lord instituted the Passover so that they would remember His power and purpose. When they crossed the Jordan into the Promised Land, He instructed them to erect stones as a memorial of His provision and promises. Jesus instituted the Lord's Supper so these visible reminders would stir fresh fidelity to the cross and gratitude for our salvation.

So, what can you leave as a visible reminder of your legacy? Some keep a handwritten journal over the years. Mine is typed in a Word format but will be left behind someday. I also wrote journals to each of my kids as they were growing up. They received them upon graduation from college. Others leave a simple notebook of thoughts. Selected "great moment" images with commentary in some form can serve this purpose. For a visual impact, others have chosen a timeless video message. Capturing this "deeper life" renewal process and your application of the eight questions might also be a priceless reminder of what your life stood for.

Commit to a Focus on the Finish Line and Beyond

I've had the privilege of traveling with Pastor Jim Cymbala, who has led The Brooklyn Tabernacle for four decades. We co-sponsor one-day events for pastors in various cities, speaking to leaders about prayer and trying to encourage them in their ministries. Often Jim quotes 1 Corinthians 3:12–15, where the work of our lives is described as "gold, silver, precious stones" as compared to "wood, hay, [and] straw." Then the passage says,

> Each one's work will become clear; for the Day will declare it, because it will be revealed by fire; and the fire will test each one's work, of what sort it is. If anyone's work which he has built on it endures, he will receive a reward. If anyone's work is burned, he will suffer loss; but he himself will be saved, yet so as through fire.

Pastor Cymbala notes that we will not be judged on the quantity of our work, but the quality of our efforts. He reflects on the fact that many of us will likely be met with the question from Jesus when we arrive in heaven, "What WERE you doing down there?"

Too often, our lifestyle and legacy fails to reflect Christ's purpose and falls short of the criterion of His reward.

In recent years, numerous writers have published accounts of their visits to heaven via their own death experiences, only to be called back to earth. Without commenting on the legitimacy of these books, I think we would do well to ask, "What will really matter one minute after I die?" And, "What commentary do I want to hear from my Savior in that instant?" Hearing the words "*What were you doing down there?*" should not be our goal.

I have been inspired countless times by the final ink that flowed to the parchment from Paul's heart as he left his summary expression of legacy to his son in the faith, Timothy. Once again, in his final words of personal testimony to his disciples, and to us, Paul wrote:

> For I am already being poured out as a drink offering, and the time of my departure is at hand. I have fought the good fight, I have finished the race, I have kept the faith. Finally, there is laid up for me the crown of righteousness, which the Lord, the righteous Judge, will give to me on that Day, and not to me only but also to all who have loved His appearing.
>
> 2 Timothy 4:6–8

If I were to summarize Paul's words to our hearts in light of the issue of legacy, it would be:

"Make your whole life a life of worship. Then, when you die, even your final breath will be an expression of God's worth. Life's a battle to be finished. Life's a race to be run all out until you hit the line. Life is about God's truth, to be cherished and embraced until your final breath. The Lord always does what is right, and He is the final judge. Keep your eyes fixed on Him always, in a vital and loving relationship. I promise you . . . it may not always be easy, but it is always worth it."

The ultimate goal of our legacy is the "Well done!" commendation of our Christ in eternity. The earthly benefit of our legacy is that we inspired those who knew us to embrace the same goal, walking along the path that has been made clear by the footprints we leave behind.

A Deeper Life Story

When most people think of legacy, family comes to mind. They aspire to pass on their family heritage or leave a lasting investment in their children. For me, legacy has a different meaning, but one that inspires much of what I do today.

Growing up in a bicultural Korean–American world provided a unique background. Because my parents emigrated to the U.S. from South Korea, I was raised in a very traditional Korean home. But as soon as I walked out the door I was a regular Westerner. My home environment included rice for all three meals. We enjoyed regular servings of kimchi, observed Korean holidays, and spoke Korean in the home. While I cherish my heritage, these cultural traditions have not carried over into my adult journey and would not be core to my personal legacy.

As a never-married single adult in my mid-forties, a life centered in biological children is not the focus of my legacy. While I enjoy close relationships with friends who have children, I have been able to focus my personal spiritual investment in other areas.

Over the years, my interaction and application of the eight questions in this book have motivated me to embrace the idea of legacy with fresh clarity. As a follower of Christ, I am able to pursue a meaningful vision for what the Lord has for my life that transcends a biological family. This is a legacy unique to me.

God has given me a passion to pursue the Great Commandment to love the Lord my God with all that I am, then to love others through unselfish service (Matthew 22:36–40). My Savior has implanted a burning desire to serve a vital role in fulfilling His Great Commission to make disciples of all nations (Matthew 28:16–20). As I pursue these dreams, I see His work in and through me to leave a legacy that lasts.

The apostle Paul wrote openly of the value of being unmarried in order to care for the things of the Lord with a singular desire to please Him (1 Corinthians 7:32). This reality has enabled me to serve as paid staff and as a volunteer at some of the most influential churches in the U.S. I have been able to travel and serve in missions endeavors in dozens of countries. Even today, I work for an international mission organization, hosting scores of people every year on cross-cultural ministry trips. I've also known the joy of pouring my life into countless young women in a discipleship relationship.

Regardless of our cultural background or marital status, we all must realize that life is short in comparison to eternity. We have to make some important choices in this journey. My deepest desire in life is to hear the Lord's "Well done!" when I enter His presence in heaven. I have resolved to live in a way that inspires those who know me to embrace the same goal, walking along the path that has been made clear by the example I leave behind.

—Sally Misook Hahn, mission mobilizer

Epilogue

The great thing is to be found at one's post as a
child of God, living each day as though it were
our last, but planning as though our world might
last a hundred years.[1]

—*C. S. Lewis*

Rejoice, O young man, in your youth,
And let your heart cheer you in the days of your youth;
Walk in the ways of your heart,
And in the sight of your eyes;
But know that for all these
God will bring you into judgment.
Therefore remove sorrow from your heart,
And put away evil from your flesh,
For childhood and youth are vanity.
Remember now your Creator in the days of your youth,
Before the difficult days come,
And the years draw near when you say,
"I have no pleasure in them."

Ecclesiastes 11:9–12:1

I want to close with a story that former U.S. Senate Chaplain
Richard S. Halverson once related about living a deeper, more
intentional life.

You're going to meet an old man someday down the road—ten,
thirty, fifty years from now—waiting there for you. You'll be catch-
ing up with him.

What kind of old man are you going to meet? He may be a seasoned, soft, gracious fellow—a gentleman who has grown old gracefully, surrounded by hosts of friends, friends who call him blessed because of what his life has meant to them. Or he may be a bitter, disillusioned, dried-up old buzzard without a good word for anyone—soured, friendless, and alone.

That old man will be you. He'll be the composite of everything you do, say, and think—today and tomorrow. His mind will be set in a mold you have made by your beliefs. His heart will be turning out what you've been putting into it. Every little thought, every deed goes into this old man.

Every day in every way you are becoming more and more like yourself. Amazing but true. You're beginning to look more like yourself, think more like yourself, and talk more like yourself. You're becoming yourself more and more.

Live only in terms of what you're getting out of life, and the old man gets smaller, drier, harder, crabbier, more self-centered. Open your life to others, think in terms of what you can give, your contribution to life, and the old man grows larger, softer, kindlier, and greater.[2]

This same wisdom, applicable to both men and women, has been expressed before but in fewer words: "Do not be deceived, God is not mocked; for whatever a man sows, that he will also reap" (Galatians 6:7). As you come to the end of this book, the real journey begins.

I sincerely hope some significant seeds of truth have been planted deep within the soil of your heart. Theology. Identity. Purpose. Values. Priorities. Goals. Time. Legacy. May they bring forth the fruit of a life well lived so at the end of your earthly travels, you'll find yourself completely ready to step through the doorway of eternity.

My prayer for you, my friend, is the same as was Paul's hope for the Colossian believers. I pray you will be filled with the knowledge of God's will in all spiritual wisdom and understanding, so that you may walk in a manner worthy of the Lord, to please Him in all respects, bearing fruit in every good work and increasing in the knowledge of God. I pray for the daily fruit of worship, integrity, and nonconformity. The fruit of a deeper life.

May God in His infinite patience and grace bring forth these
pearls of truth in the days that are before you.

Part Two

DISCOVERY EXERCISES

Theology Discovery
Exercises

How do I take the ocean of biblical truth about God and distill it down to my thimble of understanding? Among all the attributes and names of God, which do I focus on for the sake of daily renewal?

The goal of these Theology Discovery Exercises is to enable you to write out your personal theology statement in answer to the question "Who is God?" You will ultimately review this statement regularly as a foundation for your personal renewal and daily "WIN." For an example of what this might look like, see appendix 2.

- **Exercise One** will encourage you to identify positive experiences God has used to reveal the truth of His character to you in the course of your journey.

- **Exercise Two** will help you identify negative challenges and struggles that require a renewed understanding of the relevance and power of God in the midst of your daily journey.

- **Exercise Three** provides a worksheet to help you begin to craft some personal statements about the relevance of key truths about God to your daily life.

- **Exercise Four** is the final step of writing out your actual summary of your personal theology.

Exercise One: Great Moments Revealing Lessons on God's Character

One principle in knowing God's will is to learn to trust your great moments. Just as Israel memorialized their great moments of God's movement (Passover, crossing the Jordan River, etc.), we should capture and remember the lessons we have learned about God from those amazing times when He worked unmistakably in our lives.

Thinking over your journey, what have been some of those great moments when God worked powerfully in your life? What did you learn about His character? Write a summary paragraph about each one of these experiences, and then try to describe what God revealed to you about His character. Consider the following moments in your life, but add others as you think of them.

Life Experience	Lesson About God's Character
Before salvation: Describe times when you sensed God at work, revealing himself to you and drawing you to the cross.	
At salvation: Describe the experience of committing your life to Christ, including any special circumstances or truths that stood out.	
Early faith years: What particular lessons or experiences seem most compelling as you think of your early days as a follower of Christ?	
Major decisions: Think of major decisions you have faced in your life. Describe specific details and challenges.	

Personal trials or crises: Describe a season where a particular trial, circumstance, or problem seemed to test your faith or provide a powerful teaching moment.	
Marriage life: If married, describe significant lessons you have learned in your relationship.	
Family journey: As you think about your family of origin or your immediate family today, what experiences stand out?	
Ministry challenges: In your journey of serving Christ, whether vocationally or as a volunteer, what lessons or experiences have most influenced you?	

Exercise Two: Negative Challenges Requiring Affirmation of God's Character

Review the list of common personal struggles. Rank each one from 1 to 5, with 1 being never and 5 being frequent.

_____ Addictions		_____ Craving Comfort	
_____ Anger		_____ Critical	
_____ Anxiety		_____ Depression	
_____ Apathy		_____ Discontent	
_____ Bitterness		_____ Discouragement	
_____ Broken Relationships		_____ Dishonesty	
_____ Controlling		_____ Doubt	
_____ Coveting		_____ Fear	

_____ Gluttony   _____ Pride

_____ Greed   _____ Selfishness

_____ Insecurity   _____ Self-Doubt

_____ Isolation   _____ Self-Promotion

_____ Laziness
                                  _____ Starved for Attention
_____ Loneliness
                                  _____ Stressed/Overwhelmed
_____ Lust/Sensuality
                                  _____ Uncertainty
_____ Materialism
                                  _____ Unkindness
_____ Moodiness
                                  _____ Unloving
_____ Negativity

APPLICATION: Identify six or seven struggles that ranked the highest for you. Using the following list, select one of the attributes of God associated with that struggle. When you write your personal theology statement in Exercise Three, consider the attributes you have identified here. This will allow you to experience a daily renewal in the truth of God's character in order to overcome common personal struggles.

My Struggles—His Character

Addictions—Omnipotent, Gracious, Holy

Anger—Long-Suffering, Sovereign, Merciful, Forgiving

Anxiety—Sovereign, Omniscient, Wise, Good

Apathy—Holy, Faithful, Long-Suffering, Loving

Bitterness—Forgiving, Gracious, Merciful, Kind, Long-Suffering

Broken relationships—Forgiving, Gracious, Merciful, Long-Suffering

Controlling—Sovereign, Trustworthy, Peace

Coveting—All-Sufficient, Good, Just, Provider

Craving Comfort—Good, Omniscient, Omnipresent

Critical—Gracious, Forgiving, Merciful, Loving

Depression—Joy, All-Sufficient, Faithful

Discontent—Good, All-Sufficient, Wise

Discouragement—Faithful, Omniscient, Good

Dishonesty—Truth, Immutable, Holy, Righteous

Doubt—Truth, Omniscient, Immutable, Wise

Fear—Sovereign, Good, Omniscient, Omnipotent, Omnipresent

Gluttony—Self-Control, Omnipotent

Greed—Sovereign, Good, Righteous

Insecurity—Good, Faithful, Loving, Omnipotent

Isolation—Sovereign, Omnipresent

Laziness—Omniscient, Omnipotent

Loneliness—Omnipresent, Loving, Faithful

Lust/Sensuality—Holy, Omniscient, Righteous, Omnipotent

Materialism—Eternal, Good, Faithful

Moodiness—Good, Long-Suffering, Immutable

Negativity—Good, Immutable, Sovereign

Pride—Sovereign, Holy, Omnipotent, Infinite

Selfishness—Righteous, Loving, Gracious, Merciful

Self-doubt—Truthful, Wise, Omnipotent

Self-promotion—Holy, Sovereign

Starved for Attention—Omnipresent, Omniscient, Loving

Stressed/Overwhelmed—Gracious, Just, Long-Suffering, Omnipotent, Omnipresent

Uncertainty—Sovereign, Righteous, Good, Omniscient, Immutable, Incomprehensible

Unkindness—Long-Suffering, Merciful, Gracious, Loving, Good

Unloving—Loving, Long-Suffering, Gracious, Good

Exercise Three—Applying My Personal Theology (Worksheet)

Reflecting on your answers in the previous exercises, select the names or attributes of God that seem especially relevant for your unique challenges and individual journey. Also, refer to the appendixes that describe the attributes and names of the Father, Christ, and the Holy Spirit.

Using the chart below, describe the name or title of God in the left column. In the right column, describe the difference this will make in your daily life.

God is . . . *(A name or characteristic)*	Therefore . . . *(The application of who He is)*
(Example) Sovereign	I do not have to be angry or anxious because I know He is in control and has a perfect plan for my life.

Exercise Four—Writing My Personal Theology

Now, reflecting on all of these exercises, you are ready to start writing your specific theology statement. Take time to make it your own. Use your own words. Make this something that really reflects your own journey and will be memorable for many years to come. Again, see appendix 2 for an example.

Once you have completed your Personal Theology Statement, you can transfer it to The Deeper Life Summary at the back of the book.

Identity Discovery
Exercises

The goal of the Identity Discovery Exercises is to help you reflect on your sense of identity based on your unique design and life experiences. It will help to write out a personal identity statement based on your biblical, essential identity. For an example of this, you can review the statement in appendix 9.

Exercise One: My Eternal Identity

We are all created in the image of God with an everlasting soul and a body of flesh. God desires to make us spiritually alive through an authentic relationship with Him through His Son, Jesus Christ. However, the Bible says we were born in sin. The result is spiritual death and judgment (Romans 3:9–18; Ephesians 2:1–3).

Do you know that you have been made alive by entering into a relationship with God through Christ? If so, take a moment to thank Him for the power of His salvation that has made you a completely new person.

If you are not confident that you have been made alive by entering into a relationship with God through Christ, turn to Ephesians 2:1–10. See God's description of your current spiritual condition in verses 1–3. Consider what He is able to do as seen in verses 4–10. Then turn to John 1:12–13. Ask God to do a work of grace in your heart today. Pray that He will open your eyes to your need for Him. He will enable you to turn from sin, which separates you from His life, and to receive Christ as Lord of your life. By His power, He can make you alive spiritually and give you the assurance of eternal life in His name. (See John 10:27–28; 17:3.)

Exercise Two: My Experiential Identity

Negative Experiences

During your developmental years, what factors in the world around you formed concepts that have been destructive to your sense of security and well-being (derogatory names, crisis experiences, put-downs, hurtful criticisms)? Make a list of these things.

In what ways have these formed a shaky foundation for your life?

Take time now to commit any hurt, disappointment, or confusion to the Lord. Admit to God any erroneous ideas you've adopted about Him. Confess any sinful behavior that is connected to these sinful views. Admit your need for a renewed mind and perspective toward yourself. Write your prayer on a separate sheet of paper, or begin a journal or notebook for these exercises.

Positive Experiences

Think over your life to identify the positive experiences that have shaped a sense of who you are (good family relationships, positive memories, special recognitions, unique opportunities). List some of the primary ones.

How did these positively affect your understanding of your value as a person? Summarize your thoughts.

Take time now to thank the Lord for these blessings that have been an encouragement to you. At the same time, seek His grace to confront any pride that may have resulted from these positive factors.

Now surrender both the negative and positive experiences of your life to the Lord in prayer, admitting that, while these are very real, they are only superficial factors in light of your essential identity in Christ.

Exercise Three: My External Identity

List the aspects of your external appearance that you often have not appreciated.

Read Psalm 139:13–17. Confess to God your willingness to trust the wisdom of His handiwork in making you. Thank Him for the way He has fashioned your external identity. Thank him that how you appear on the outside does not affect the value of who you are on the inside. Ask Him to take any weaknesses and use them to glorify himself by His grace (2 Corinthians 12:9–10). Write that prayer in your notebook.

List the aspects of your external appearance that you most appreciate.

Now recognize that these, too, are gifts from God's good hand. Remind yourself that He gave you these for His glory, not yours. Review 1 Samuel 16:7, Romans 12:1–2; and 1 Corinthians 6:19–20. Write down a prayer that reflects these verses as it relates to your external person.

Finally, thank God that in this image-oriented society, His love for you is in no way affected by your appearance. You are loved from the inside out, not the outside in.

Exercise Four: My Essential Identity

Review the list (appendix 8) of "Who I Am in Jesus Christ." Thank God that every one of these things is true—He has said so. Take time to list the truths that especially counteract the negative inputs of your past or motivate you toward the future.

Now begin to craft a biblical "Identity Statement" that incorporates some of these truths and expresses who you really are.

Exercise Five: My Effective Identity

Begin now to think about your S-DNA (Spiritual DNA).

Spiritual gifts—Review Romans 12:6–8; 1 Corinthians 12:1–31; and 1 Peter 4:7–11. List the gifts that seem to interest you or the ones that you've seen active in your life.

Write down the ways in which you have served the Lord in the church and have seen a supernatural result in people's lives.

You may want to take one (or both) of the following free spiritual gifts assessments and then summarize your results.

http://www.cpcsda.org/uploads/Spiritual-Gifts-Inventory.pdf

http://exchristian.net/images//wagner_modified_houts.pdf (longer version)

Desires of the heart—Write down the areas of involvement or service that you tend to gravitate toward and which, when you are involved, are very rewarding.

Natural talents—Write down some of your natural abilities, which can be used to honor God as He empowers them.

Aptitudes (temperament, learning, and communication styles)— Write down some of your personality strengths and weaknesses (ask the opinion of friends or co-workers who will be honest with you).

How do you usually learn most effectively (by seeing examples, by listening, by asking questions, by reading, by writing)?

How do you best function when working with a group of people?

Ask some friends this question: "What shows up when I show up?" (the good, the bad, and the ugly). My friend and life coach, Michal Pfau, describes this as your "essence"—the spirit of who you are, which alters or changes the energy and mood of the room when you enter. It is your personal signature or impression that arrives. This is like your favorite fragrance/cologne, except it is unique to you. You don't recognize it because it is always the way it is when you are around. You may want the person to get the description down to one or two words (fun, warmth, direction, leadership, etc.). If you did this exercise, what did you discover?

Try taking some personality assessments, such as:

- People Map personality profile, available online http://www
  .peoplemapsystem.com. Or order a hard copy from Life
  Coach Michael Pfau—mike@crosswayslifecoaching.com.
  (A cost is associated with these assessments.)

- DISC Personality Assessment: Free short version: http://disc personalitytesting.com/free-disc-test/. (A longer version is available on the same site but has a cost associated with it.)
- Talents, Aptitude, Leadership, and Learning style: http:// www.crgleader.com/assessments-and-solutions. (A cost is associated with this assessment.)
- The Strengths Finder 2.0 is another excellent assessment that can be utilized with the purchase of the book. For more information, see: http://strengths.gallup.com/purchase.aspx. (A cost is associated with this assessment.)

Now review the various answers you gave to the above questions or discovered through your assessments, and summarize your aptitudes.

Your S-DNA Overview: Try to write a summary based on the exercises above:

My Spiritual Gifts are:

My Desires are:

My Natural Talents are:

_____

_____

_____

_____

My Aptitudes (personality and approach) are:

_____

_____

_____

_____

Using these conclusions, complete The Deeper Life Summary in the back of the book and review regularly.

Purpose Discovery
Exercises

The goal of the Purpose Discovery Exercises is to help you write down your own clear and compelling statements about your specific purposes. At a minimum, you will want to have a clear Earthly Purpose (or mission) that you can consistently review.

Your Eternal Purpose

You are no doubt familiar with the Westminster Catechism statement "The chief end of man is to glorify God and enjoy Him forever." This reflects the purpose behind our very existence now and in eternity.

Now review chapter 3, describing our eternal purpose. Write a statement about God's eternal purpose for your life. (It could be similar to the Westminster Catechism statement but modified to reflect your own thoughts.)

Your Earthly Purpose (Mission)

Review the idea of an earthly purpose or mission, in chapter 3, and complete the following exercises.

Christ's Purpose: Read the following passages, which describe Christ's earthly purpose (or mission): Matthew 5:17; 20:28; Luke 4:43; 12:19; 19:10; John 3:14–15; 9:39; 10:10; 12:47; 18:37; 1 Timothy 1:15. What specific elements of Christ's mission seem especially meaningful to your life? Write them down.

Your Life's Summary: If you could write a summary paragraph of your life that would someday be chiseled on your tombstone, what would it say?

Express Your Theology and Identity: Go back and review your theology statement and your *essential* and *effective* identity summaries. With those in mind, what thoughts do you have about your unique purpose on this earth as a specific expression of your theology and identity?

Using your reflections in the previous three exercises, write a mission statement describing your earthly purpose for being here right now in this lifetime. Title it "My Earthly Purpose/Mission." Once you have completed it to your satisfaction, enter it in The Deeper Life Summary section at the back of the book.

Your Explicit Purposes

Review the discussion on the explicit purposes of your life in chapter 3.

Using the chart below, list the key roles and relationships you fulfill in life. In the adjoining space, begin to craft a purpose statement for each function.

Role:	Purpose:
Example: **Mother**	My purpose as a mother is to teach my children to love God. Therefore, I will seek to raise them with no regrets, modeling and instructing them in godliness and putting their interests above my own.

Now complete The Deeper Life Summary in the back of the book to allow you to see the connection and flow of your specific answers to the longings of your soul.

Values Discovery
Exercises

The goal of the Values Discovery Exercises is to help you discover and write out the key values that you will review regularly in order to guide the implementation of your purposes in life.

You can complete these exercises using the space provided here in the book or by utilizing a separate piece of paper or a Word document. In any case, writing your answers will be important for clarification.

Formulating Your DECLARED Values

Reflecting on your stated convictions: Write brief descriptions of the convictions you determine to be most important in your life. These are principles that you hope you would never compromise in the course of daily living. This is a brainstorming type of exercise, so be open and creative as you write.

Researching the Word: Take some time to clarify the key passages of Scripture that have most influenced your life. These may be favorite verses from childhood. Perhaps they will be verses that have been vital in past decisions. Maybe they will be fairly recent discoveries from your reading. Write down the references along with a brief description of the values taught in each passage. Example:

Bible Reference:

Core Value in This Verse:

1 Corinthians 13

Love is the motivation and measure of all I do.

Revisit your "most admired" list: Write down the names of the people who have most influenced you in your life. These people may be parents, spiritual leaders, friends, or associates. Some may be heroes from many years ago whose biographies have touched you at a deep level. Next to each name, write the virtues that stand out. (Don't forget to consider the life and character of the Lord Jesus Christ. He is our ultimate model.) Example:

I admire:

Because . . .

Uncle Steve

He has endured hardship with grace and hope.

Receive honest feedback: Tell some trusted friends or relatives what you are working on. Ask them to be specific and honest with you. Find out from their perspective what they would say are your guiding principles in life based on the way you have lived before them. Record their answers.

Ready to synthesize: Now review the lists you have made in the previous exercises. Look for recurring themes. Notice values that are similar and can be combined. Try to summarize the results. Hopefully you can end up with a list of five, ten, or fifteen "declared" core values that you can begin to clarify for your own list.

Investigating Your DEMONSTRATED Values

Along the way you will want to take time for a "reality check." Our ideals guide us toward a higher level of living. However, we often live below those ideals because our affections are set on lesser things. Remember the simple equation:

Declared values − demonstrated values = hypocrisy

Here are some steps to assess your demonstrated values before you actually finalize the process by writing your values down:

- What dominates my thoughts? What do I really spend most of my time thinking about? Write these down.
- Where do I spend my time? Time is life. If our time is spent on things that do not reflect our declared values, we have dissonance. Write down the things that dominate your time each day.
- How do I spend my money? Where your treasure is, there will your heart be also. In honesty, write down what your bank statement tells you about your values.
- How do I react? Review what we said about reactions in this chapter. What do my reactions reveal about the values that motivate me?
- What would a brutally honest friend or associate say? Imagine their answers. Or, if you are really ready for some "reality," ask them. What demonstrated values do they see in your life that may be negative, destructive, or contradictory in comparison to your declared values?
- In a spirit of humble dependence upon God, review your DECLARED VALUES (in the first part of this exercise) and compare them to your DEMONSTRATED VALUES (in the second part). Then seek His grace to deal with any contradictions you discover. Use this as a time to reaffirm your declared values that are supported by your demonstrated values and trust God for power to live accordingly.

Organize to Memorize

This final step may take some time. You may want to organize your selected values into a form that will be easy to remember and apply at any moment to your life. It may be an acrostic, where the first letters of the words are arranged to spell something. It may be in alphabetical order. You may choose alliteration, where all the words begin with the same letter. It's up to you.

Once you are satisfied with your written values, transfer your ideas to The Deeper Life Summary at the back of the book.

Priorities Discovery
Exercises

The goal of this section is to guide you in identifying the key commitments you need to focus on in the core areas of your life.

We have defined *priorities* as the commitments we put first because we believe they are important.

It is important to clarify the most important commitments. You cannot do everything, but you can certainly do the best things. The table below lists the six guideposts described in this chapter. (Review the descriptions as needed.)

Across the top you will want to fill in the various "roles and relationships" you identified under your "Explicit Purposes." Examples would be: "Christ-Follower; "Spouse"; "Parent"; "Employee"; "Sunday School Teacher"; "Little League Coach." Obviously, you may need more than three columns to complete this exercise. Feel free to use a separate piece of paper or a Word document.

Remember, your explicit purposes describe "why" God has you in particular roles and relationships. Priorities describe "what" you need to focus on most intently in order to fulfill those purposes.

This is a brainstorming activity. You may put a lot of ideas in the various boxes. After you have filled in this chart, take time to review, synthesize, and organize your ideas. The net result will be a list of the priorities you will want to commit yourself to and keep in focus.

When you have finished this exercise and clarified core priorities, you can enter the results in The Deeper Life Summary at the end of the book.

This is an exercise that should be done at least once a year to make certain that you are integrating your priorities with the other vital issues in your life.

Remember, these commitments are based on your values, purpose, identity, and theology. Review the foundational components of your priorities often.

Assessing Your Priorities

	Role or Relationship	Role or Relationship	Role or Relationship
Scripture: What commitments matter most according to Scripture?			
Stewardship: What commitments best utilize my "S-DNA"?			
Servanthood: What commitments will best meet the needs of those I am called to serve?			
Significance: What commitments will advance God's kingdom and matter most in eternity?			

Satisfaction:
What com-
mitments
will be most
rewarding
based on my
foundations?

Stability:
What com-
mitments will
bring balance
and well-
being over the
long haul?

Based on the assessment above, use this chart to write down your specific and most important commitments you will seek to pursue and protect on a daily basis. These are the yeses that will empower you to say *no* to distractions and demands that might dilute your effectiveness in each area.

Articulating Your Priorities

Personal Life Priorities	Family Life Priorities	Work Life Priorities	Ministry Life Priorities

Finally, transfer these key priorities to The Deeper Life Summary at the back of the book and move to the next exercises to create specific goals for each priority.

Goals Discovery
Exercises

U se these questions as a guide to developing good goals. You will need to refer to this page for developing goals to fulfill each priority you identified in the last chapter.

My Priority

Write the priority these goals will accomplish.

Goals (Rough Draft)

Write down at least three goals you will need to aim toward in order to achieve this priority. This will be a rough draft, so don't scrutinize too much at this point.

Step One: Consecration

What areas of my life will I have to surrender to God in order to accomplish these goals? (Review Proverbs 16:1–4.)

Am I willing to make the sacrifices necessary to pursue these goals?

Step Two: Preparation

Are these goals specific? In what ways? If not, write specifics that ought to be clarified.

Are these goals measurable? If not, put some measuring mechanisms in place for each one. How will I know when I am on course? How will I know if my pace is on target for accomplishing these goals?

Are these goals attainable? What will keep me from attaining these goals? Is it realistic to overcome the hindrances? If not, adjust the ambition of the goal. If the hindrances can be overcome, how will I do that?

Step Three: Imagination

In what ways will these goals require faith?

What positive outcomes will occur if I achieve these goals? Write these down.

What promises of God's Word will I focus on to keep my faith growing?

When and how will I systematically pray about these targets?

Step Four: Execution

Now write a final version of your goals, having completed the first three steps.

Step Five: Evaluation

(Complete this step once a month.)

Are these goals still integrated and consistent with the foundations of theology, identity, purpose, values, and priorities? If not, how can I make adjustments?

Am I on target with the established measurements? If not, how can I make adjustments to stay on course?

How am I, by faith, regularly trusting God for these goals?

Step Six: Celebration

(To be completed just before the goals are met.)

How will I celebrate the accomplishment of these goals? When will this occur? Who will I include?

How can I give praise and thanksgiving to God for this achievement?

After this evaluation, write your goals that are attached to each priority in The Deeper Life Summary at the back of the book.

Time Discovery
Exercises

These exercises are designed to be used on a regular basis as you construct and/or evaluate your schedule.

Exercise One: Evaluating the Minutes (*Chronos*)

Periodically, take time to look at your schedule, using the ten quick tips described in appendix 13. Make note of any adjustments you need to make or items for which you need to plan. Note any insights you gain about your week as you prayerfully complete this exercise.

Exercise Two: Experiencing the Moments (*Kairos*)—"Finding *Kairos* in the Chaos of your *Chronos*"

Column 1 lists the days of the week. Columns 2 and 3 identify the two areas in which *kairos* often occurs. In these columns, note the minutes that could become moments with a few key words to describe how this might happen. Reflect on some of your key goals as well. This can be done for a few weeks, to get in the habit, and periodically thereafter. Note the samples given to get you started.

Day of the week:	Eternal moments w/ your eternal God (renewal)	Eternal moments w/ eternal souls (reproduction)
Sample: Tuesday: Work day, evening meeting at church Other opportunities to look for: • pray w/people on the phone • pray through newspaper as I read about events • remember key goal of praying with three people per day	*In shower* (5:30 a.m.): Review memory verses; sing praises. *Driving out of neighborhood:* Pray for neighbors who need Christ. *Driving home* (5:00 p.m.): Pray for the children and families from my fifth grade class at church. *Dinner with my spouse:* Read from devotional book after dinner. *Children's ministry volunteer meeting:* Encourage the group to stop and pray about agenda items before moving to next discussion.	*Morning work break* (9:30 a.m.): Remind Steve that my husband and I have been praying for his wife's health issues. *Lunch w/ Susan* (noon): Encourage her to join my Sunday night small group. *Children's ministry meeting:* Catch Laurie at the break and pray about her wayward son.
Sunday: Other notes:		
Monday : Other notes:		
Tuesday: Other notes:		

Wednesday: Other notes:		
Thursday: Other notes:		
Friday: Other notes:		
Saturday: Other notes:		

Having completed this exercise, write a few key statements about your time commitments in The Deeper Life Summary at the back of the book.

Legacy Discovery
Exercises

The goal of these exercises is to help you clarify the kind of legacy you want to leave when your journey on this earth is done. Just as you have done in previous exercises, you will want to enter your clarified answers in The Deeper Life Summary.

Two Letters

End of Life: Remembering that "an inheritance is what we leave *for* people and a legacy is what we leave *in* them." Take some time to write an "end of life" letter. Imagine it is the last hour of your life. Address the letter to the most important people of your journey. Describe what you hope you left *in* them. As you write, consider these themes: What do I want others to remember about me? What opportunities and risks have enriched my life? What has God's blessing looked like during my journey? What regrets must I surrender and trust to the mercy of God? Be as honest and specific as possible.

After you finish the letter, ask yourself: "What do I need to focus on every day in order for this letter to be an authentic representation of my legacy?"

First Minute in Heaven: Imagine you have just arrived in heaven. Based on all you know from the Bible, imagine this new experience. Write a "first minute in heaven" letter. Address the letter to the Lord. What are you feeling about Him at this moment? What are you glad you did while you were on earth? What do you hope

He will say to you and about you? What might you wish you had done on earth before this moment in eternity?

After you finish the letter, ask yourself: "What do I need to focus on every day in order for this letter to be a letter of complete joy and ultimately honoring to my Lord?"

Ten People

Review the key elements of a positive legacy, as noted in chapter 8. Using the chart below, list the key categories of people in whom you would like to leave a legacy (examples: spouse, children, grandchildren, co-workers, fellow believers, neighbors). Remembering the two letters you wrote, write a short description of what you want this legacy to look like.

Name/Relationship	Your Legacy in Their Lives

Finally, use The Deeper Life Summary to add your specific desires for leaving a legacy.

Acknowledgments

We've all prepared an entire lifetime for this moment. Similarly, this book is the culmination of a lifetime of relationships, experiences, and discoveries—converging in the clarification of ideas. So I must try, in summary form, to say thanks.

First, I thank God for the dark days of my journey that have caused the light of His truth revelations to spring freshly from the pages of Scripture, leading to this renewal process that has transformed my life.

Of course, I am deeply grateful to my wife, Rosemary, for joining me on this journey for over thirty years. Not only has she endured the expedition but she has encouraged me to write about it in ways that I hope will help many others.

Countless fellow believers have inspired me to persevere in the continued development of the renewal principles presented in these pages. As I have preached these truths, presented seminars, and written specifically about this process over the years—their testimonies have helped me realize the value of this approach. I wish I could thank each of you personally for so passionately applying this approach and demonstrating the impact through your lives.

Pat Roberts, an insightful Christ-follower and skilled writer, first inspired me to put this process into written form back in the mid-nineties after hearing me preach about the relevance of these questions. I will always be indebted to her for her skill and support in effectively sharing this approach with thousands, literally all around the world.

Finally, Brenda Brown, another skilled writer and passionate mom and wife, has helped me significantly in the editing and improvement of this manuscript. I believe this is just the beginning of her writing ministry as she continues to write and bless others with her insights through her personal projects in the days ahead. You can enjoy her blog at http://momofinfluence.com.

Appendix 1

God's Self-Revelation

Some truths about God may at first seem to discourage us in our attempts to know Him:

- Heaven is His throne and earth is His footstool. There is no way we could ever build a place or system of worship to contain Him (Isaiah 66:1).

- He is Spirit, ultimately existing beyond what we can contain in any physical, tangible sense.

- He is the God "who alone has immortality, dwelling in unapproachable light, whom no man has seen or can see" (1 Timothy 6:16).

Yet in His determination that we would know Him in this earthly journey, He has communicated His character to us in a variety of terms.

Anthropomorphic—These terms represent images associated with our humanness. For example, anthropomorphic terms describe God as a king, lord, judge, lawgiver, potter, father, mother, lover, healer, teacher, shepherd, provider, protector, servant, and friend. The Bible also describes the eyes, mind, heart, arm, feet, and hand of the Lord. Of course, He has none of these physical attributes, but His Word uses their function to make His work and ways clear to us.

Non-anthropomorphic—These descriptions represent images that are non-human, but ones that we can readily understand. For instance, we read about God as a shield, fortress, rock, fire, light, eagle, lion, bear, mother hen, cloud, wind, and breath.

Relational—Using our common understanding of relationships, God describes himself as loving, merciful, good, truthful, wise, gracious, forgiving, tender, long-suffering, humble, just, wise, and righteous. In absolute perfection He is, at times, also wrathful and jealous.

Transcendent—Some of His attributes transcend our human experience but are clear in His self-revelation, to incite worship in our hearts. The Bible says He is all-powerful, all-knowing, all-present, perfect in holiness, eternal, unchanging, infinite, sovereign, self-existent, entirely self-sufficient, and ultimately incomprehensible.

Appendix 2

My Personal Theology Statement

My God is the **CREATOR**.

So I will rest in knowing that all of life has divine design and spiritual purpose.

My God is absolutely **SOVEREIGN**.

So I will be still and know that He is God, assured that He is firmly in charge, even when life seems out of control.

My God is completely **GOOD**.

So I can choose to live in His peace and joy, even when circumstances and people seem bad.

My God is always **JUST**.

So I will commit my soul to Him who judges righteously, even when life looks and feels unfair.

My God is unconditional in His **LOVE**.

So I will anchor my well-being in the truth that nothing that happens and nothing I do can cause Him to love me any more or any less.

My God is abundant in **GRACE**.

So I will receive His tailor-made grace for everything I face, knowing He will empower me in my weaknesses and forgive me in my failures—and enable me to do the same for others.

My God is **HOLY**.

So I can surrender myself as a living sacrifice to the One whose absolute moral purity is untainted by this sinful world.

My God is **ALL-KNOWING**.

So I will live in transparency and authenticity, knowing there is no motive, thought, or detail of my life about which He is unaware.

My God is **ALL-POWERFUL**.

So I will rest in His sufficiency with the confidence that there is no personal struggle or life problem beyond His capability of handling with ease.

My God is **ALL-PRESENT**.

So I will seek to live for an audience of one, knowing there is no secret place in my world apart from His comforting peace and holy presence.

My God is completely **WISE**.

So I will trust in the Lord with all my heart, assured that He has all the answers to any question or issue that perplexes me.

My God is **THE LORD JESUS CHRIST**.

So I will seek to know and be like Him, convinced that He is the perfect and radiant picture of God. He is the Savior, model, and Master of my life.

My God lives in me by the **HOLY SPIRIT**.

So I will consistently and humbly surrender to His control, assured that He is my constant companion, performing a perfect and powerful ministry of encouragement, guidance, and teaching in and through my life for Christ's glory.

Appendix 3

My Lord
Jesus Christ

My Jesus is the . . .

Light of the World, so I will invite His warmth and radiance into all the dark and cold places of my life so that He might expose and cleanse my sin and selfishness.

Only Wise God, so I can boldly ask and receive from Him all necessary insight, guidance, and direction for my life today.

Rock of My Salvation, so I will rest secure and safe, knowing that He has already done everything to save me and to keep me in His love forever.

Desire of All Nations, so I will passionately proclaim his truth and beauty in every place, expressing to others the delight I have found in Him.

Justifier, so I do not have to work today to be accepted by God, but can simply live in the grace that has made me pure and lovely in His sight.

Emmanuel, so I will enjoy and practice His wonderful presence in my life today, knowing that He is with me always.

Strength of My Soul, so I come to Him in humility, delighting in my weaknesses, that His power may be demonstrated through me in every situation I encounter.

Unchanging Friend, so I will enjoy His faithful companionship and rest securely in his always-reliable love and commitment to me.

Savior, so I will kneel before His cross in grateful worship and will live by faith in the One who loved me and gave himself for me.

Cornerstone, so I will confidently base my well-being on the truth of who He is and allow Him to build my life by His strength and stability.

Healer of My Soul, so I will come to Him with all my hurts, disappointments, and fears to receive His supernatural touch of wholeness, encouragement, and peace.

Resurrection and the Life, so I will let Him live through me today in the triumph He has already achieved over all sin and death.

Image of the Invisible God, so I will draw near and gaze upon Him in intimacy today that He might reveal the fullness of the Father, Son, and Holy Spirit to my heart.

Shield of My Salvation, so I will trust Him today to protect my faith and to preserve my life in Him by His promise and power.

Truth, so I will come to Him with all my doubts and questions, receiving counsel from His reliable Word and consolation from His Spirit in order to live in this world with confidence.

Appendix 4

The Attributes of God

Eternal—God has no beginning, and He is not confined to the finiteness of time or of man's reckoning of time. He is, in fact, the cause of time. (Deuteronomy 32:40; Isaiah 57:15; Revelation 1:8)

Faithful—God is always true to His promises. He can never draw back from His promises of blessing or of judgment. Since He cannot lie, He is totally steadfast to what He has spoken. (Deuteronomy 7:9; Psalm 146:6; 2 Timothy 2:13)

Good—Because God is good, He gives to others with no ulterior motive, nor is He limited by what the recipients deserve. (2 Chronicles 5:13; Psalm 106:1; Nahum 1:7)

Gracious—Our God is a forgiving God. His goodness and compassion cause Him not to treat us as our sins deserve but instead to provide the way for our salvation. (Nehemiah 9:31; Isaiah 30:18; 2 Corinthians 9:8; Ephesians 1:6)

Holy—God is a morally excellent, perfect being. His is purity of being in every aspect. (Leviticus 19:2; Isaiah 47:4, 57:15; 1 Peter 1:15)

Immutable—God is always the same in His nature, His character, and His will. He never changes, and He can never be made to change. (Numbers 23:19; Psalm 102:25–27; Malachi 3:6; Hebrews 13:8)

Impartial—The Lord of the universe does not show favoritism or partiality. He does not treat any one of us as our sins deserve but freely offers His grace to all. (Deuteronomy 10:17; Job 34:19; Romans 10:12; 1 Peter 1:17)

Incomprehensible—Because God is God He is beyond the understanding of man. His ways, character, and acts are higher than ours. We only understand as He chooses to reveal himself. (Job 11:7; Isaiah 55:8–9; Romans 11:33)

Infinite—God has no space/time limits or bounds whatsoever. (1 Kings 8:27; Psalm 145:3)

Jealous—God is unwilling to share His glory with any other creature or give up His redeemed people. His holiness does not tolerate competitors or those who sin against Him. (Exodus 20:5; 34:14; Joshua 24:19)

Just—God is fair in all His actions. Whether He deals with man, angels, or demons, He acts in total equity by rewarding righteousness and punishing sin. Since He knows all, every decree is absolutely just. (Numbers 14:18; Psalm 89:14; Romans 3:25–26)

Long-Suffering—God's righteous anger is slow to be kindled against those who fail to listen to His warnings or to obey His instructions. The eternal longing for the highest good for His creatures holds back His holy justice. (Exodus 34:6–7; Psalm 78:38; 2 Peter 3:9)

Loving—Because God is a loving God, He freely gives himself for others, even laying down His life for us all. He desires for others the highest good without any thought for himself. This love is not based on the worth, response, or merit of the one being loved. (1 Chronicles 16:34; Jeremiah 31:3; Romans 5:8; 1 John 4:7–11)

Merciful—God is an actively compassionate being. He responds in a compassionate way toward those who have oppressed His will in their pursuit of their own way. (Deuteronomy 4:31; Psalm 62:12, Micah 7:18; Romans 9:14–16)

Omnipotent—God possesses all power. He is able to bring into being anything that He has decided to do with or without the use of any means. (Genesis 18:14; Job 42:2; Jeremiah 32:27; Ephesians 3:20–21)

Omnipresent—God is present everywhere in all the universe, at all times, in the totality of His character. (Psalm 139:7–10; Proverbs 15:3; Jeremiah 23:23–24; Hebrews 4:13)

Omniscient—God knows all. He has perfect knowledge of everything that is past, present, or future. (Job 37:16; Psalm 139:1–6; Proverbs 5:21; Romans 11:33)

Righteous—God is always good. He always does the right thing. Whatever He does is right. He is the absolute. His actions are always consistent with His character, which is love. (Deuteronomy 32:4; Psalm 119:142; Hosea 14:9; Matthew 5:48)

Self-Existent—God depends on nothing else for His existence; the whole basis of His existence is within himself. Before creation, there was nothing *but* God himself. He added nothing to himself by creation. (Exodus 3:14; John 5:26)

Sovereign—God is totally, supremely, and preeminently over all His creation. There is not a person or thing that is not under His control and foreknown plan. (Job 9:12; Psalm 99:1; Daniel 4:35; Acts 4:24–28)

Transcendent—God is above His creation, and He would exist if there were no creation. His existence is totally apart from His creatures or creation. (Isaiah 43:10; 55:8–9)

Truthful—Everything God says is reality. Whether believed by man or not, whether seen as reality or not, if it is spoken by God, it is reality. Whatever He speaks becomes truth as we know it. (1 Samuel 15:29; Psalm 31:5; Titus 1:2; 1 John 5:20)

Wise—God's actions are based on His character, which allows Him to choose righteous ends and to make fitting plans to achieve those ends. (Job 12:13; Isaiah 40:28; Daniel 2:20; James 3:17)

Wrathful—God hates all that is unrighteous and has an unquenchable desire to punish all unrighteousness. Whatever is inconsistent with Him must ultimately be consumed. (Exodus 34:6–7; 2 Chronicles 19:2; Romans 1:18; Hebrews 10:30–31)

(Adapted from *Lord, I Want to Know You* by Kay Arthur, Waterbrook Press, 2000)

Appendix 5

The Old Testament Names of God

Those who know Your name will put their trust in You; for You, LORD, have never forsaken those who seek You.

—Psalm 9:10

ADONAI—The Lord (Genesis 15:2; Psalms 123:2; 135:5; 136:3; 145:14–15; Matthew 10:34–40; Luke 14:25–27; John 13:13–16; Romans 10:8–10)

ELOHIM—The Creator (Genesis 1:1, 26–27; Psalm 139:13–14; Isaiah 43:7; Colossians 1:16)

EL ELYON—The God Most High (Genesis 14:19–20; 1 Samuel 2:6–10; Isaiah 14:24, 27; 46:9–11)

EL ROI—The God Who Sees (Genesis 16:13; Psalm 139:7–12; 2 Thessalonians 1:3–10)

EL SHADDAI—The All-Sufficient One (Genesis 17:1–8; 2 Corinthians 12:9–10)

JEHOVAH—The Self-Existent One (Genesis 2:4; Exodus 3:13–15; 34:5–7; Hebrews 13:8; Revelation 1:8; 22:13)

JEHOVAH-JIREH—The Lord Will Provide (Genesis 22:8, 14; Isaiah 31:1; Matthew 6:11; John 3:36; 5:21; Romans 8:32; 10:13; Philippians 4:19; Hebrews 9:27–28)

JEHOVAH-MEKODDISHKEM—The Lord Sanctifies You (Exodus 19:2–6; 31:13; Leviticus 20:26; Ephesians 5:25–27; 1 Thessalonians 5:23; Hebrews 10:10–14; 12:14)

JEHOVAH-NISSI—The Lord Your Banner (Exodus 14:13; 17:15–16; Deuteronomy 20:3–4; 1 Samuel 15:16–23; Hebrews 7:25)

JEHOVAH-QANNA—The Lord Who Is Jealous (Exodus 20:1–6 ; 34:12–17)

JEHOVAH-RAAH—The Lord My Shepherd (Psalms 23:1–6; 100:3; Isaiah 53:6; Ezekiel 34:11; John 10:1–17, 27; 21:17)

JEHOVAH-RAPHA—The Lord Who Heals (Exodus 15:22–27; 2 Kings 20:1, 4–5; 2 Chronicles 7:14; Isaiah 19:22; 53:5; Jeremiah 8:22; Luke 4:18; 1 Peter 2:24–25)

JEHOVAH-SABAOTH—The Lord of Hosts (1 Samuel 1:1–3; 17:42–47; Jeremiah 20:11–13; Malachi 1:10–11, 14)

JEHOVAH-SHALOM—The Lord Is Peace (Leviticus 26:2–6; Isaiah 26:3; Jeremiah 29:11; Psalm 119:165; Romans 5:33; Philippians 4:4–7)

JEHOVAH-SHAMMAH—The Lord Is There (Exodus 13:20–22; 23:20–22; 33:12–15; Joshua 1:5; John 14:2–3)

JEHOVAH-TISIDKENU—The Lord Our Righteousness (Jeremiah 23:6; Matthew 5:20; Romans 3:21–22; 6:16; 2 Corinthians 5:21)

Appendix 6

Titles and Names of Jesus

We know of more than one hundred names and titles for Jesus. Listed here are a number of them. As you go over this list, note that they describe the character of Jesus, the greatness of His glory and power, and also how He came to earth as a servant to provide you with many blessings.

Scriptures used are from *The World English Bible*.

ADAM: 1 Corinthians 15:45, "So also it is written, 'The first man, Adam, became a living soul.' The last Adam became a life-giving spirit."

ALMIGHTY: Revelation 1:8, "'I am the Alpha and the Omega,' says the Lord God, 'who is and who was and who is to come, the Almighty.'"

ALPHA and OMEGA: Revelation 22:13, "I am the Alpha and the Omega, the First and the Last, the Beginning and the End."

AMEN: Revelation 3:14, "To the angel of the assembly in Laodicea write: 'The Amen, the Faithful and True Witness, the Head of God's creation, says these things: "I know your works, that you are neither cold nor hot. I wish you were cold or hot."'"

APOSTLE: Hebrews 3:1, "Therefore, holy brothers, partakers of a heavenly calling, consider the Apostle and High Priest of our confession, Jesus." (The word *apostle* should be translated *messenger*.)

AUTHOR AND PERFECTER OF FAITH: Hebrews 12:2, "Looking to Jesus, the author and perfecter of faith, who for the joy that was set before him endured the cross, despising shame, and has sat down at the right hand of the throne of God."

AUTHOR OF SALVATION: Hebrews 2:10, "For it became him, for whom are all things, and through whom are all things, in bringing many children to glory, to make the author of their salvation perfect through sufferings."

BLESSED AND ONLY RULER: 1 Timothy 6:15, "In its own times he will show, who is the blessed and only Ruler, the King of kings, and Lord of lords."

BREAD OF LIFE: John 6:48, "I am the bread of life."

BRIGHT and MORNING STAR: Revelation 22:16, "I, Jesus, have sent my angel to testify these things to you for the assemblies. I am the root and the offspring of David; the Bright and Morning Star."

CHIEF SHEPHERD: 1 Peter 5:4, "When the chief Shepherd is revealed, you will receive the crown of glory that doesn't fade away."

CHRIST OF GOD: Luke 9:20, "He said to them, 'But who do you say that I am?' Peter answered, 'The Christ of God.'"

COUNSELOR: Isaiah 9:6, "For to us a child is born. To us a son is given; and the government will be on his shoulders. His name will be called Wonderful, Counselor, Mighty God, Everlasting Father, Prince of Peace."

CREATOR: Colossians 1:16, "For by him were all things created, in the heavens and on the earth, things visible and things invisible, whether thrones or dominions or principalities or powers; all things have been created through him, and for him."

DELIVERER: Romans 11:26, "And so all Israel will be saved. Even as it is written, 'There will come out of Zion the Deliverer, and he will turn away ungodliness from Jacob.'"

DOOR: John 10:7–9, "Jesus therefore said to them again, 'Most certainly, I tell you, I am the sheep's door. All who came before me are thieves and robbers, but the sheep didn't listen to them. I am the door. If anyone enters in by me, he will be saved, and will go in and go out, and will find pasture.'"

EVERLASTING FATHER: Isaiah 9:6, "For to us a child is born. To us a son is given; and the government will be on his shoulders. His name will be called Wonderful, Counselor, Mighty God, Everlasting Father, Prince of Peace."

FAITHFUL WITNESS: Revelation 1:5, "And from Jesus Christ, the faithful witness, the firstborn of the dead, and the ruler of the kings of the earth. To him who loves us, and washed us from our sins by his blood."

FIRST AND LAST: Revelation 1:17, "When I saw him, I fell at his feet like a dead man. He laid his right hand on me, saying, 'Don't be afraid. I am the first and the last.'"

FIRSTBORN: Revelation 1:5, "And from Jesus Christ, the faithful witness, the firstborn of the dead, and the ruler of the kings of the earth. To him who loves us, and washed us from our sins by his blood."

GOD: 1 Timothy 2:5, "For there is one God, and one mediator between God and men, the man Christ Jesus."

GOOD SHEPHERD: John 10:11, "I am the good shepherd. The good shepherd lays down his life for the sheep."

GOVERNOR: Matthew 2:6, "'You Bethlehem, land of Judah, are in no way least among the princes of Judah: for out of you shall come a governor, who shall shepherd my people, Israel.'"

GREAT HIGH PRIEST: Hebrews 4:14, "Having then a great high priest, who has passed through the heavens, Jesus, the Son of God, let us hold tightly to our confession."

HEAD OF GOD'S CREATION: Revelation 3:14, "To the angel of the assembly in Laodicea write: 'The Amen, the Faithful and True Witness, the Head of God's creation, says these things.'"

HEAD OF THE ASSEMBLY: Ephesians 1:22, "He put all things in subjection under his feet, and gave him to be head over all things for the assembly."

HEIR OF ALL THINGS: Hebrews 1:2, "God, having in the past spoken to the fathers through the prophets at many times and in various ways, has at the end of these days spoken to us by his Son, whom he appointed heir of all things, through whom also he made the worlds."

HOLY SERVANT: Acts 4:27, "For truly, in this city against your holy servant, Jesus, whom you anointed, both Herod and Pontius Pilate, with the Gentiles and the people of Israel, were gathered together."

HOLY AND RIGHTEOUS ONE: Acts 3:14, "But you denied the Holy and Righteous One, and asked for a murderer to be granted to you."

HOLY ONE OF GOD: Mark 1:24, "What do we have to do with you, Jesus, you Nazarene? Have you come to destroy us? I know you who you are: the Holy One of God!"

HORN OF SALVATION: Luke 1:68–69, "Blessed be the Lord, the God of Israel, for he has visited and redeemed his people; and has raised up a horn of salvation for us in the house of his servant David."

I AM: John 8:58, "Jesus said to them, 'Most certainly, I tell you, before Abraham came into existence, I AM.'"

IMAGE OF GOD: 2 Corinthians 4:4, "The god of this world has blinded the minds of the unbelieving, that the light of the Good News of the glory of Christ, who is the image of God, should not dawn on them."

IMMANUEL: Isaiah 7:14, "Therefore the Lord himself will give you a sign. Behold, the virgin shall conceive, and bear a son, and shall call his name Immanuel."

JESUS: Matthew 1:21, "She shall bring forth a son. You shall call his name Jesus, for it is he who shall save his people from their sins."

KING ETERNAL, IMMORTAL, INVISIBLE: 1 Timothy 1:17, "Now to the King eternal, immortal, invisible, to God who alone is wise, be honor and glory forever and ever. Amen."

KING OF THE JEWS: Matthew 2:2, "Where is he who is born King of the Jews? For we saw his star in the east, and have come to worship him."

KING OF KINGS: 1 Timothy 6:15, "In its own times he will show, who is the blessed and only Ruler, the King of kings, and Lord of lords."

KING OF THE NATIONS: Revelation 15:3, "They sang the song of Moses, the servant of God, and the song of the Lamb, saying, 'Great and marvelous are your works, Lord God, the Almighty! Righteous and true are your ways, you King of the nations.'"

LAWGIVER: Isaiah 33:22, "For Yahweh is our judge. Yahweh is our lawgiver. Yahweh is our king. He will save us."

LAMB: Revelation 13:8, "All who dwell on the earth will worship him, everyone whose name has not been written from the foundation of the world in the book of life of the Lamb who has been killed."

LAMB OF GOD: John 1:29, "He saw Jesus coming to him, and said, 'Behold, the Lamb of God, who takes away the sin of the world!'"

LIFE: John 14:6, "Jesus said to him, 'I am the way, the truth, and the life. No one comes to the Father, except through me.'"

LIGHT OF THE WORLD: John 8:12, "Jesus spoke to them, saying, 'I am the light of the world. He who follows me will not walk in the darkness, but will have the light of life.'"

LION OF THE TRIBE OF JUDAH: Revelation 5:5, "One of the elders said to me, 'Don't weep. Behold, the Lion who is of the tribe of Judah, the Root of David, has overcome; he who opens the book and its seven seals.'"

LORD: John 20:28, "Thomas answered him, 'My Lord and my God!'"

LORD OF ALL: Acts 10:36, "The word which he sent to the children of Israel, preaching good news of peace by Jesus Christ—he is Lord of all."

LORD OF GLORY: 1 Corinthians 2:7–8, "We speak God's wisdom in a mystery . . . which none of the rulers of this world has known. For had they known it, they wouldn't have crucified the Lord of glory."

LORD OF LORDS: 1 Timothy 6:15, "In its own times he will show, who is the blessed and only Ruler, the King of kings, and Lord of lords."

MAN OF SUFFERING: Isaiah 53:3, "He was despised, and rejected by men; a man of suffering, and acquainted with disease. He was despised as one from whom men hide their face; and we didn't respect him."

MEDIATOR: 1 Timothy 2:5, "For there is one God, and one mediator between God and men, the man Christ Jesus."

MESSENGER OF THE COVENANT: Malachi 3:1, "Behold, I send my messenger, and he will prepare the way before me; and the Lord, whom you seek, will suddenly come to his temple; and the messenger of the covenant, whom you desire, behold, he comes!"

MESSIAH (THE ANOINTED ONE): Daniel 9:25, "Know therefore and discern, that from the going out of the commandment to restore and to build Jerusalem to the Anointed One, the prince, shall be seven weeks, and sixty-two weeks: it shall be built again, with street and moat, even in troubled times." John 1:41, "He first found his own brother, Simon, and said to him, 'We have found the Messiah!'"

MIGHTY GOD: Isaiah 9:6, "For to us a child is born. To us a son is given; and the government will be on his shoulders. His name will be called Wonderful, Counselor, Mighty God, Everlasting Father, Prince of Peace."

NAZARENE: Matthew 2:23, "[Mary and Joseph] came and lived in a city called Nazareth; that it might be fulfilled which was spoken through the prophets: 'He will be called a Nazarene.'"

OUR PASSOVER: 1 Corinthians 5:7, "Purge out the old yeast, that you may be a new lump, even as you are unleavened. For indeed Christ, our Passover, has been sacrificed in our place."

PRINCE OF PEACE: Isaiah 9:6, "For to us a child is born. To us a son is given; and the government will be on his shoulders. His name will be called Wonderful, Counselor, Mighty God, Everlasting Father, Prince of Peace."

PROPHET: Luke 24:19, "He said to them, 'What things?' They said to him, 'The things concerning Jesus, the Nazarene, who was a prophet mighty in deed and word before God and all the people.'" Acts 3:22, "For Moses indeed said to the fathers, 'The Lord God will raise up a prophet for you from among your brothers, like me. You shall listen to him in all things whatever he says to you.'"

REDEEMER: Job 19:25, "But as for me, I know that my Redeemer lives. In the end, he will stand upon the earth."

RESURRECTION AND LIFE: John 11:25, "Jesus said to her, 'I am the resurrection and the life. He who believes in me will still live, even if he dies.'"

RIGHTEOUS ONE: Acts 7:52, "Which of the prophets didn't your fathers persecute? They killed those who foretold the coming of the Righteous One, of whom you have now become betrayers and murderers."

ROCK: 1 Corinthians 10:4, "All drank the same spiritual drink. For they drank of a spiritual rock that followed them, and the rock was Christ."

SAVIOR: Luke 2:11, "For there is born to you today, in David's city, a Savior, who is Christ the Lord."

SHEPHERD AND OVERSEER: 1 Peter 2:25, "For you were going astray like sheep; but are now returned to the Shepherd and Overseer of your souls."

SON OF DAVID: Matthew 1:1, "The book of the genealogy of Jesus Christ, the son of David, the son of Abraham."

SON OF MAN: Matthew 8:20, "Jesus said to him, 'The foxes have holes, and the birds of the sky have nests, but the Son of Man has nowhere to lay his head.'"

SON OF THE MOST HIGH: Luke 1:32, "He will be great, and will be called the Son of the Most High. The Lord God will give him the throne of his father, David."

TRUE LIGHT: John 1:9, "The true light that enlightens everyone was coming into the world."

TRUE VINE: John 15:1, "I am the true vine, and my Father is the farmer."

TRUTH: John 14:6, "Jesus said to him, 'I am the way, the truth, and the life. No one comes to the Father, except through me.'"

WAY: John 14:6, "Jesus said to him, 'I am the way, the truth, and the life. No one comes to the Father, except through me."

WITNESS: Isaiah 55:4, "Behold, I have given him for a witness to the peoples, a leader and commander to the peoples."

WONDERFUL: Isaiah 9:6, "For to us a child is born. To us a son is given; and the government will be on his shoulders. His name will be called Wonderful, Counselor, Mighty God, Everlasting Father, Prince of Peace."

WORD: John 1:1, "In the beginning was the Word, and the Word was with God, and the Word was God."

WORD OF GOD: Revelation 19:13, "He is clothed in a garment sprinkled with blood. His name is called 'The Word of God.'"

YAHWEH: Isaiah 26:4, "Trust in Yahweh forever; for in Yah, Yahweh, is an everlasting Rock."

YAHWEH OUR RIGHTEOUSNESS: Jeremiah 23:6, "In his days Judah shall be saved, and Israel shall dwell safely; and this is his name by which he shall be called: Yahweh our righteousness."

(Adapted from http://www.abetterhope.com/whois/titles.html)

Appendix 7

Names of the Holy Spirit

Author of Scripture: (2 Peter 1:21; 2 Timothy 3:16) The Bible is inspired, literally "God-breathed," by the Holy Spirit, the third person of the Trinity. The Spirit moved the authors of all sixty-six books to record exactly what He breathed into their hearts and minds. As a ship is moved through the water by wind in its sails, so the biblical writers were borne along by the Spirit's impulse.

Comforter/Counselor/Advocate: (Isaiah 11:2; John 14:16; 15:26; 16:7) All three words are translations of the Greek *parakletos,* from which we get *Paraclete,* another name for the Spirit. When Jesus went away, His disciples were greatly distressed because they had lost His comforting presence. But He promised to send the Spirit to comfort, console, and guide those who belong to Christ. The Spirit also "bears witness" with our spirit that we belong to Him, thereby assuring us of our salvation.

Convicter of Sin: (John 16:7–11) The Spirit applies the truths of God to people's own minds in order to convince them by fair and sufficient arguments that they are sinners. He does this through the conviction in our hearts that we are not worthy to stand before a holy God, that we need His righteousness, and that judgment is certain and will come to all people one day. Those who deny these truths rebel against the conviction of the Spirit.

Deposit/Seal/Earnest: (2 Corinthians 1:22; 5:5; Ephesians 1:13–14) The Holy Spirit is God's seal on His people, His claim on us as His very own. The gift of the Spirit to believers is a down payment on our heavenly inheritance, which Christ has promised us and secured for us 227 at the cross. It is because the Spirit has sealed us that we are assured of our salvation. No one can break the seal of God.

Guide: (John 16:13) Just as the Spirit guided the writers of Scripture to record truth, so does He promise to guide believers to know and understand that truth. God's truth is "foolishness" to the world, because it is "spiritually discerned" (1 Corinthians 2:14). Those who belong to Christ have the indwelling Spirit who guides us into all we need to know in regard to spiritual matters. Those who do not belong to Christ have no "interpreter" to guide them to know and understand God's Word.

Indweller of Believers: (Romans 8:9–11; 1 Corinthians 6:19; Ephesians 2:21–22) The Holy Spirit resides in the hearts of God's people, and that indwelling is the distinguishing characteristic of the regenerated person. From within believers, He directs, guides, comforts, and influences us, as well as producing in us the fruit of the Spirit (Galatians 5:22–23). He provides the intimate connection between God and His children. All true believers in Christ have the Spirit residing in their hearts.

Intercessor: (Romans 8:26) One of the most encouraging and comforting aspects of the Holy Spirit is His ministry of intercession on behalf of those He inhabits. Because we often don't know what or how to pray when we approach God, the Spirit intercedes and prays for us. He interprets our "groanings," so that when we are oppressed and overwhelmed by trials and the cares of life, He comes alongside us to lend assistance as He sustains us before the throne of grace.

Revealer/Spirit of Truth: (John 14:17; 16:13; 1 Corinthians 2:12–16) Jesus promised that after the resurrection, the Holy Spirit would come to "guide you into all truth." Because of the Spirit in our hearts, we are able to understand truth, especially in spiritual matters, in a way that non-Christians cannot. In fact, the truth the Spirit reveals to us is "foolishness" to them, and they cannot understand it. But we have the mind of Christ in the person of His Spirit within us.

Spirit of God/the Lord/Christ: (Matthew 3:16; 2 Corinthians 3:17; 1 Peter 1:11) These names remind us that the Spirit of God is indeed part of the triune Godhead and that He is just as much God as the Father and the Son. He is first revealed to us at the creation, when He was "hovering over the waters," denoting His part in creation, along with that of Jesus who made all things (John 1:1–3). We see this same Trinity of God again at Jesus' baptism, when the Spirit descends on Jesus and the voice of the Father is heard.

Spirit of Life: (Romans 8:2) The term *Spirit of life* means the Holy Spirit is the one who produces or gives life, not that He initiates salvation but rather that He imparts newness of life. When we receive eternal life through Christ, the Spirit provides the spiritual food that is the sustenance of the spiritual life. Here again, we see the triune God at work. We are saved by the Father through the work of the Son, and that salvation is sustained by the Holy Spirit.

Teacher: (John 14:26; 1 Corinthians 2:13) Jesus promised that the Spirit would teach His disciples "all things" and bring to their remembrance the things He said while He was with them. The writers of the New Testament were moved by the Spirit to remember and understand the instructions Jesus gave for the building and organizing of the church, the doctrines regarding himself, the directives for holy living, and the revelation of things to come.

Witness: (Romans 8:16; Hebrews 2:4; 10:15) The Spirit is called "witness" because He verifies and testifies to the fact that we are children of God, that Jesus and the disciples who performed miracles were sent by God, and that the books of the Bible are divinely inspired. Further, by giving the gifts of the Spirit to believers, He witnesses to us and the world that we belong to God.

(Adapted from http://www.gotquestions.org/names-Holy-Spirit.html#ixzz2S4AQCHBO)

Appendix 8

Who I Am in Jesus Christ

I am the salt of the earth. (Matthew 5:13)

I am the light of the world. (Matthew 5:14)

I am a child of God, part of His family. (John 1:12; Romans 8:16)

I am part of the true vine, a channel of Christ's life. (John 15:1, 5)

I am Christ's friend. (John 15:15)

I am chosen and appointed by Christ to bear His fruit. (John 15:16)

I am a son of God. God is spiritually my Father. (Romans 8:14–15; Galatians 3:26; 4:6)

I am no longer under condemnation, because I am in Christ. (Romans 8:1)

I am a joint heir with Christ, sharing His inheritance with Him. (Romans 8:17)

I am accepted by Christ and belong in His family. (Romans 15:7; Ephesians 1:6)

I am sanctified, set apart for His use. (1 Corinthians 1:2)

I am a temple (home) of God. His Spirit (His life) dwells in me. (1 Corinthians 3:16; 6:19)

I am a member (part) of Christ's body. (1 Corinthians 12:27; Ephesians 5:30)

I am a new creation in Christ. (2 Corinthians 5:17)

I am reconciled to God and am an ambassador for Christ. (2 Corinthians 5:18–20)

I am the righteousness of God because of Christ. (2 Corinthians 5:21)

I am a son of God and one with other believers in Christ. (Galatians 3:26, 28)

I am an heir of God since I am a son of God. (Galatians 4:6, 7)

I am a saint. (1 Corinthians 1:2; Ephesians 1:1; Philippians 1:1; Colossians 1:2)

I am blessed with every spiritual blessing. (Ephesians 1:3)

I am chosen, holy, and blameless before God. (Ephesians 1:4)

I am secure and sealed by the power of the Holy Spirit. (2 Corinthians 1:22)

I am God's workmanship (handiwork) created (born anew) in Christ to do His work that He planned beforehand that I should do. (Ephesians 2:10)

I am a fellow citizen with the rest of God's people in His family. (Ephesians 2:19)

I am righteous and holy. (Ephesians 4:24)

I am a citizen of heaven and seated in heaven right now. (Ephesians 2:6; Philippians 3:20)

I am hidden with Christ in God. (Colossians 3:3)

I am an expression of the life of Christ because He is my life. (Colossians 3:4)

I am chosen of God, holy, and dearly loved. (Colossians 3:12)

I am a son of light and not of darkness. (1 Thessalonians 5:5)

I am a partaker of Christ, and I share in His life. (Hebrews 3:14)

I am one of God's living stones being built up (in Christ) as a spiritual house. (1 Peter 2:5)

I am a chosen race, a royal priesthood, a holy nation, a people for God's own possession to proclaim His praises. (1 Peter 2:9–10)

I am an alien and stranger to this world I temporarily live in. (1 Peter 2:11)

I am an enemy of the devil. (1 Peter 5:8)

I am a child of God. When Christ returns, I will be like Him. (1 John 3:1–2)

I am born of God and the evil one (the devil) cannot touch me. (1 John 5:18)

(Adapted from *Living Free in Christ* by Neil Anderson, Gospel Light Publishers, 1993)

My Identity

Here is an example of the specific identity statements you are encouraged to create through the Discovery Exercises. As you write your purpose statements in The Deeper Life Summary at the back of the book, perhaps this will provide some inspiration.

MY ESSENTIAL IDENTITY

I, Daniel D. Henderson, am a new creature in Jesus Christ—a completely loved, fully accepted, and totally empowered child of the most living, most high, most holy God. I have been created by His amazing grace for a life full of good works and God's glory through Christ my Lord.

MY EFFECTIVE IDENTITY
(Spiritual DNA)

I am most effective when . . .

I exercise my spiritual gifts of . . .

- Leadership
- Teaching/Preaching
- Faith
- Serving

I express my deepest desires for . . .

- Training/Encouraging leaders
- Catalyzing renewal for churches/Christians
- Influencing others in prayer
- Speaking/Motivating
- Long-term impact through writing
- Advancing global missions

I utilize my natural talents of . . .

- Speaking
- Singing/Worship
- Creativity
- Integration
- Relating to people

I fulfill my unique aptitudes for . . .

- Task-orientation
- Results-orientation
- Entrepreneurship
- Extroversion

My Strengths Finder Results: Strategic, Activator, Futuristic, Command, Belief

Myers-Briggs Assessment Results: ENTJ (Extrovert, Intuitive, Thinking, Judging)

Appendix 10

The Henderson Family Values

As you prepare to clarify your family values in written form in The Deeper Life Summary section, here is an example of values that have worked for us over the years.

Principle One
(*Spirituality*)
Love God with all your heart.
(Matthew 22:37–38)

Principle Two
(*Service*)
Serve and love other people.
(Matthew 22:39–40; Galatians 5:13–14)

Principle Three
(*Renewal*)
Pray and read your Bible every day.
(Matthew 4:4; 1 Thessalonians 5:17)

Principle Four
(*Obedience*)
Please and obey God—no matter what.
(2 Corinthians 5:9; 1 Samuel 15:22)

Principle Five
(*Honesty*)
Always tell the truth.
(Ephesians 4:15, 25; Psalm 15:1–2)

Principle Six
(*Credibility*)
Always keep your word.
(Psalm 15:4)

Principle Seven
(*Endurance*)
Finish what you start.
(2 Timothy 4:7; Hebrews 12:1–2)

Principle Eight
(*Self-Management*)
Use your time wisely.
(Ephesians 5:15–16; Psalm 39:4)

Principle Nine
(*Excellence*)
Always look your best.
(1 Corinthians 6:19–20)

Principle Ten
(*Dependence*)
Pray for wisdom every day.
(1 Kings 3:9–10; Proverbs 2:1–8; James 1:5)

Principle Eleven
(*Purity*)
Always have a pure mind, a grateful heart,
and a clear conscience.
(Philippians 4:8; 1 Timothy 1:4;
1 Thessalonians 5:18)

Principle Twelve
(*Enthusiasm*)
Give it all you've got!
(Ecclesiastes 9:10; 1 Corinthians 15:58;
Colossians 3:23–24)

Appendix 11

Personal Values

As you prepare to clarify your personal values in written form in The Deeper Life Summary section, here is my personal example that might serve as a springboard for your list. You will notice that I utilized my first name to help me recall my values more readily.

Discipline—Everyone thinks of changing the world. No one thinks of changing himself. Discipline allows me to begin the change with me and accept responsibility for my choices. I will regulate my conduct by principle rather than by emotion, impulse, or convenience. As Zig Ziglar said, "When you do the things you ought to do when you ought to do them, the day will come when you will do the things you want to do when you want to do them." (1 Timothy 4:7–8; 2 Timothy 1:7; 2 Peter 1:5–6)

Attitude—My attitude determines my altitude. Each day I will trust God for the grace to live by faith—with optimism and hopefulness. This will result in a spirit of encouragement, affirmation, and celebration in my interaction with others. (Proverbs 23:7, Philippians 2:1–4; James 3:17–18)

Nonconformity—I will not go where the path may lead. I will go instead where there is no path and leave a trail. This will involve the regular habit of seeing the world through eyes of faith—risking, adventuring, and trusting God for new and meaningful exploits. (Romans 12:1–2; Hebrews 11:6)

Integrity—I will live a life where all the pieces fit together, springing from a heart of self-honesty and resulting in personal, interpersonal, and financial blamelessness. (Psalm 15; 1 Timothy 3:1–4; Acts 20:28)

Excellence—The Lord's name is excellent so I will trust Him for the grace to live, work, and play in a fashion that brings honor to Christ and speaks well of His work in me. If something is worth doing, it is worth doing right. (Psalm 8:9; Ecclesiastes 9:10; 1 Corinthians 15:58; Colossians 1:10)

Love—Love is an act of self-sacrifice, flowing from the heart, by the power of the Spirit, for the good of others and the glory of God. If love is not my motive and means, I am nothing. The earthly impact and eternal reward of all of my actions depend on this primary desire in life. (Matthew 22:37–40; 1 Corinthians 13: 1–4, 13; 1 Timothy 1:5)

Appendix 12
Five Ministry Priorities

As you prepare to clarify your ministry priorities in written form in The Deeper Life Summary section, here is one example of such a listing.

In attempting to live externally the priorities that have been decided internally, I have clarified *five priorities* in my own ministry. I want to be what God wants me to be and do what I think God wants me to do. It may not be what others think I should be doing, but as long as it is my conviction to please God, I seek to *maintain, master, model, multiply,* and *mobilize* within these clarified decisions.

Maintain an Exemplary Life (1 Timothy 3:2–7; 4:12, 16; Acts 20:18–21; 1 Peter 5:3; 1 Corinthians 11:1; Philippians 4:9; Titus 2:7–8). This has to be first, as I focus on my spiritual, emotional, mental, physical, marital, family, and relational health. Without it, my credibility and ministry will fail. Example is your most powerful rhetoric.

Master the Study of God's Word (Acts 6:2; 1 Timothy 4:6, 13–15; 5:17; 2 Timothy 2:15; 4:1–2). The conviction to "study to show [myself] approved unto God" (KJV) ultimately results in a depth of life that makes my message authentic. "Son of man, let all my words sink deep into your own heart first. Listen to them carefully for yourself. Then go to your people . . ." (Ezekiel 3:10–11 NLT).

Model a Commitment to Prayer Mark 1:35; Luke 6:12; 9:28; 11:1; 22:39; Acts 1:14; 6:4; Romans 15:30; Colossians 1:3; 4:2). The prayer level of any ministry never rises any higher than the personal example and passion of the primary leader. I cannot point the way—I must lead the way.

Multiply Leadership Within the Church (John 17:6–20; Acts 10:17–38; Ephesians 4:11–12; 2 Timothy 2:2). Leaders don't fall from trees. Future generations of spiritual leadership are only developed through intentional, biblical, and transparent equipping of the hearts and minds of emerging leaders.

Mobilize the Church Toward Missions (Matthew 28:18–20; Mark 16:15; John 20:21; Acts 13:1–3; Philippians 3:12–17; 2 Timothy 4:5–8). Stephen Covey said, "The main thing is to keep the main thing the main thing." Because the Holy Spirit is the "how-to" of ministry, I must seek His mind, will, and direction for the ministry, involving others with me in prayer, fasting, and full surrender of the fabric and future of the ministry to Him.

Quick Tips on Time Management

Let me give you a very quick summary of ten practical ideas for trying to develop some good habits in your expenditure of the stewardship of life. This is a perspective on how to better understand and control the minutes, hours, and days of your earthly pilgrimage.

1. Realization

The Bible tells us that our life is a vapor. Not too impressive or enduring, is it. We "appear" for a moment, then vanish away. The older I get, the more I realize that this earthly journey is at best a brief appearance.

That's the practical reality that prompted the psalmist to pray, "Lord, make me to know my end, and what is the measure of my days, that I may know how frail I am. Indeed, You have made my days as handbreadths, and my age is as nothing before You; certainly every man at his best state is but vapor" (Psalm 39:4–5). The first practical step to time management is to realize how little of it we really have and how quickly it will run through our fingers like sand.

2. Preparation

It has been said many times that people don't plan to fail, they just fail to plan. This principle applies to everyday time decisions. A few minutes spent planning in the morning before rushing out the door with the cereal bowl in your hand and your shoes untied will save you headaches later. It has been said that ten minutes spent in planning will save at least an hour during the day. That's good stewardship.

3. Standardization

You can usually tell how disorganized someone is by how many different sizes and types of paper they use to write things down—or how many "to do" lists they have on their computers, iPads, or smartphones. That is where a standardized planning system helps immensely. Fortunately, there are an abundance of apps available today that help make this a reality.

4. Delegation

In a commitment to mutual effectiveness and growth, share the load with others. It is important to look through your tasks and time commitments and ask, "Is there anyone who can accomplish this as well as I can?"

We often suffer under erroneous conclusions about the issue of delegation. We think we don't have time to delegate. In reality, we don't have time to do otherwise. A small investment of time spent in training will pay large rewards in the long run. Busy mothers can employ children much more than they often do in accomplishing chores around the house. Learn to let go of the need for perfectly made beds and neatly folded clothes. How will our children learn unless we give them an opportunity? At home, work, or in ministry, it is always a pleasant surprise to witness the positive fruit of delegation. As skills are developed, people often excel in handling delegated responsibilities, freeing up your time to focus on goals more significant to your unique calling.

5. Communication

Time management is a team effort. We often forget that we are

interdependent with others in what we do with our time. I have found that spending time explaining my schedule and plans to my family, staff, and friends is a great help in the long run. They are able to give me solid and realistic feedback. I find that they are also more sensitive to the value of my time as I try to be a good steward each day.

6. Evaluation

Periodically, it is important to look back as well as ahead. While tedious, we all need to track how we have spent a day by keeping a log. Try it for a week. Then make a serious investigation into how your activities matched your plans and accomplished your goals. Gurus on the matter of time almost universally agree on the importance of this exercise on an occasional basis.

7. Elimination

Bill Yeager, an amazing pastor, now in heaven, used to say, "Every healthy body needs a good elimination system." Of course, this is true about our physical body. (He actually used this idea in reference to churches.) This statement is also true with reference to our calendars. You can't add important obligations without removing the less important items. Eliminating time commitments is not always easy or popular. It's easier to add than to subtract. But reducing your obligations is essential. Goals, priorities, values, purpose, identity, and theology will guide you in what to eliminate.

8. Adaptation

I often quote verses from a book I like to call "Second Daniel." It is my book-in-progress featuring "Danielisms" from my sermons over the years. One of my favorite beatitudes from this book reads, "Blessed are the flexible, for they shall not be broken." A similar verse states, "The only branches that don't bend are the dead ones." The book of Proverbs says, "The heart of man plans his way but 245 the Lord directs his steps." Since God is the owner of our time, we need to be sensitive to His leading in executing our well-laid plans. The late Oswald Sanders highlighted this truth well: "Few things are more apt to produce agitation and tension in a busy life than unexpected and unwelcome interruptions. To Him (Christ) there were no such things as interruptions in His God-planned life."

9. Integration

Queen Elizabeth I, when facing imminent death, said, "All my possessions for a moment of time." This is how precious time is. We need to constantly remember how important it is and respond accordingly. We must take time each day to review our "foundations for living." Time spent in reviewing the eight questions in this book, and your answers to them, will guide your daily choices of time management and add meaning to the minutes of your life. This may be the difference between spending a day of your life on earth or investing a day of your life for eternity. Whether you are in the shower, sitting in a meeting, pausing for a snack, or dozing off to sleep, the battle for integrity and significance can stand or fall on these quick and quiet minutes of focus.

Napoleon once said, "There is in the midst of every great battle ten to fifteen minutes that are crucial. Take that period and you win the battle. Lose it and you'll be defeated." If we have not prepared our hearts, we may lose the battle. I find that each day brings the need for me to prepare myself for the battle of life. Time spent in answering these essential questions is the key to victory in the day-to-day stewardship of life.

10. Eternization

I had to look hard for this word. It is legitimate and means, "To make something eternal." This has to do with our time. In all things I ask myself, "What can I do in this minute or hour that will really matter in eternity?" C. S. Lewis said, "The present is the point at which time touches eternity . . . in it alone freedom and actuality are offered."[1]

Jonathan Edwards shared this good advice, both by his life and by his words: "I will never do anything which I should be afraid to do if it were the last hour of my life." He understood the importance of eternal significance.

Discussion Questions

These questions are designed for further study and interaction, based on related Bible passages, and can be used either personally or in a group context. For more information about our Deeper Life Small-Group DVD Study, visit www.strategicrenewal.com.

Introduction

1. Ours is a world of unprecedented distraction. Read the story of a good but very distracted woman in Luke 10:38–42. How was Martha distracted and why? Specifically, how have you struggled with distraction this week? How would you summarize Jesus' words of correction to Martha? How would you like this study to help you make better choices, as Mary did in this story?

2. This book challenges us to "WIN" through our worship, integrity, and nonconformity. Read Romans 11:33–12:2. How do you see worship as foundational to the teaching of this passage? How is integrity pictured here? What does nonconformity to the world look like in this passage? Why is this kind of commitment so important every day for every believer?

3. Review the eight longings described in the introduction. Which one most specifically reflects what is going on in your life right now? Why? How do you hope this study will give you guidance in finding the satisfaction of that longing in the truth of God and His Word?

Chapter One: "Who Is God?"

1. Read Exodus 3:1–4:9. In this encounter between God and Moses, what did God reveal about himself? How did this revelation change the way Moses was going to live his life? How did God keep coming back to the issue of His own identity and power to give perspective to Moses? Similarly, how has God revealed himself to you in your life? How has this changed the course of your existence here on earth?

2. Review Isaiah's encounter with God in Isaiah 6:1–8. Even though the passage is familiar, what do you observe about how Isaiah's view of God affected his sense of mission and direction in life? What did he understand about God and what specific difference did it seem to make in what he would do after this encounter?

3. Read Daniel 4:28–37. Here is a powerful, self-directed man whose encounter with God jolted his perspective of himself and his life. Make BEFORE and AFTER columns and write down the words or ideas that show the contrast caused by Nebuchadnezzar's understanding of the true God. Looking around society, how do you see people living in the BEFORE column or the AFTER column, based on their theology?

Chapter Two: "Who Am I?"

1. Read 2 Corinthians 4:16–5:10. Here Paul is reflecting on the difference between our "external" identity and our "essential" identity. What differences does he note? Because he was clear about his essential identity in Christ, what purposes and perspectives does he embrace? How about you? How much of your life is lived focusing on the external person versus the essential you and the goals of that dimension? Does anything need to change?

2. Continue with Paul as he describes how his new life in Christ affects his motives and objectives. Based upon 2 Corinthians 5:11–15, what seems to now matter most

because of this sense of identity? What now motivates him? In what ways can you adopt this motivation as your own?

3. Going on to verses 16–21, how does Paul's new life affect the way he sees other people? With this new perspective, what does he feel compelled to do about it and why? What words does Paul use in this passage to describe himself? If this is truly your self-understanding, what change of focus might you adapt this week?

Chapter Three: "Why Am I Here?"

1. Read the following verses, which describe Christ's mission here on earth: Matthew 5:17; 20:28; Luke 4:43; 12:19; 19:10; John 3:1; 9:39; 10:10; 12:47; 18:37; 1 Timothy 1:15. With these thoughts in mind, what do you think might be applicable to the one who claims to be a follower of Christ in this life? What elements of this mission do you feel you should more fully embrace and follow?

2. Read Ephesians 2:10 and Philippians 2:13. Make a list of those works that you feel God would want you to do, based on your gifts, interests, abilities, personality, and experiences. What does this do to your motivation, knowing that all these areas can be used for God's purpose? What thoughts do you have concerning the passage in Philippians relative to your works?

3. Read Romans 14:12 and 1 Corinthians 3:10–15. If you suddenly stand before the Lord, what are the things that you would be able to put on your account that would be a fulfillment of God's purpose for your life? What changes would you want to make in your present activities?

Chapter Four: "What Really Matters?"

1. Review Exodus 20:1–17. Here we see the Lord giving to Israel (and to all who would know and follow Him) a set of

principles by which to live. Review these and take a few moments to write, in your own words, a philosophy statement based upon these fundamental precepts. It doesn't have to be a perfect rendition, just a summary statement that makes sense to you. How do you actually embrace this statement in your lifestyle? Would you say this is part of your personal philosophy of life? Why, or why not?

2. Read the story in Luke 10:25–37. On a piece of paper (or on a white board if you are in a group) make a list of the key players in this story. Now, based upon their described actions, what core values do they reflect? How do these differ from first impressions based on appearance or title? Can you think of times when your actual philosophy showed in your actions, even though you may have created a different impression toward others via external means?

3. Read Matthew 19:16–24. What was this man's stated philosophy? What was his actual philosophy? Is there any apparent disparity? How do you see this same problem in people's lives today? How about your own life?

Chapter Five: "What Shall I Do?"

1. Read Matthew 6:19–24. What warning did Jesus give here about wrong priorities? What dilemma would people face if they chose this pathway of wrong priorities? What did He suggest they do to deal with the problem? Do you think the average Christian today is really committed to this kind of obedient living? Why or why not?

2. Continue reading this section by noting Matthew 6:25–34. What did our Lord challenge us to NOT focus on? Why did He say this? Do you order your priorities in this way? How might your lifestyle and priorities change today in order to reflect a strong adherence to Matthew 6:33?

3. Read the account of the Prodigal Son in Luke 15:11–22. How did the priorities of this young man become confused? What result did his decisions create? What did it take for

him to reassess? In what way do you find people today playing the role of the prodigal in their own decision-making processes, and what does it usually take to get them to reassess? What warning and reassurance does Psalm 32:2–10 give on this issue?

Chapter Six: "How Shall I Do It?"

1. Read Nehemiah 1–2. What specific goal had God established in Nehemiah's heart? Now review the passage to see what kind of theology Nehemiah embraced (1:4–11). How did he view himself? What words does Nehemiah use? How did his theology and identity affect his goal? How does your theology and identity affect your goals?

2. Continuing in these two chapters of Nehemiah, why do you suppose Nehemiah was not content to remain in Persia with King Artaxerxes? Based on the account, what kind of purpose statement might fit Nehemiah's life as his overarching objective for living? What pursuits did he reject in order to accomplish this mission? In what way have you exemplified this same kind of focus?

3. Read John 17:1–18. Here, Christ reflects on the objective and accomplishments of His ministry. Note how verses 1–5 speak of His purpose to glorify the Father and of His mission to bring eternal life. He felt he had completed this mission. From the following verses (6–18), what goals had been accomplished to achieve this sense of completion? What can you learn from the deliberate nature of His life as you clarify His goals for your life?

Chapter Seven: "When Shall I Do It?"

1. Read Mark 1:21–35. List the various activities Jesus was involved in on this particular Sabbath day in Capernaum. How did Jesus maintain a right attitude in the midst of such a high priority on spending time with His Father? Are

you taking sufficient time to meet with God and to get His direction and power for your life and ministry?

2. Read John 9:4–5. How did the realization of the shortness of His time on earth affect Jesus? What are "the works of Him who sent Me" that Jesus fulfilled while He was here on earth? What are some of the works God wants to accomplish through you during your time here on earth? How can you use your time today to do the works of Him who sent you?

3. Read John 11:1–10, 18–26, 38–45. Humanly speaking, what were some disadvantages to Jesus' waiting two days to go to Lazarus's home? What blessings and benefits occurred because Jesus was sensitive to God's perfect timing? What activities are on your "urgent" list that God may want you to wait to accomplish so He can receive greater glory? What activities are you delaying that God may want you to do immediately?

Chapter Eight: "How Will I Finish?"

1. Jesus' final words to His disciples, prior to His ascension, are recorded in Matthew 28:18–20; Luke 24:44–49; Acts 1:6–8. In many ways, this describes the legacy He had in mind for His closest followers. How would you summarize this legacy? How might your legacy reflect these same ideals? What are you doing to make it so?

2. Paul spent some final moments with the leaders of the church in Ephesus (see Acts 20:17–38). Read through this section of Scripture. List three things that seem to represent the legacy Paul left in these leaders. Now list three things he hoped would represent their legacy. As you think about this "legacy interchange," how would you like to make this kind of investment in someone else during your lifetime? Who are they? How might you give this more intentional focus in the course of your weekly schedule?

3. As this chapter notes, 2 Timothy was Paul's final letter to his "son in the faith." His final description of his legacy is found in 2 Timothy 4:6–8. How do you hope to be able to say something similar as you prepare to cross life's finish line? Specifically, what do you hope it looks like in connection to your unique journey?

The Deeper Life
Summary

Answers to the
Deepest Longings of Your Soul

On the next few pages, enter your written statements for daily renewal.

- **The FOUNDATION** section will reflect answers that seldom change, once clarified, that help you affirm your theology, identity, purposes, and values.
- **The IMPLEMENTATION** section will be dynamic as you reaffirm key priorities, establish goals to accomplish those priorities, and manage your time to achieve the goals.
- **The DESTINATION** section will inspire you to continue toward the ultimate longing to leave a legacy that really matters.

Foundation

Who Is God? (My Theology)

My God is . . .

_____

_____

_____

_____

_____

_____

Who Am I? (My Identity)

My Essential Identity:

I, _____ (name) am . . .

_____

_____

My Effective Identity: (SDNA)

I am most effective when . . .

- I exercise my spiritual gifts of . . .

_____

- I express my deepest desires for . . .

_____

- I utilize my natural talents of . . .

_____

- I fulfill my unique aptitudes of . . .

Why Am I Here? (My Purpose)

My eternal purpose is . . .

My earthly purpose is . . .

My explicit purposes are . . .

As a _____ (role), my purpose is . . .

As a _____ (role), my purpose is . . .

As a _____ (role), my purpose is . . .

As a _____ (role), my purpose is . . .

What Really Matters? (My Values)

My life values are . . .

Implementation

What Should I Do? (My Priorities)	How Should I Do It? (My Goals)
Role	Personal Goals
1.	1a.
	1b.
	1c.
2.	2a.
	2b.
	2c.
3.	3a.
	3b.
	3c.
Role	
1.	1a.
	1b.
	1c.
2.	2a.
	2b.
	2c.
3.	3a.
	3b.
	3c.

The Deeper Life Summary

What Should I Do? (My Priorities)	How Should I Do It? (My Goals)
Role	Personal Goals
1.	1a.
	1b.
	1c.
2.	2a.
	2b.
	2c.
3.	3a.
	3b.
	3c.
Role	
1.	1a.
	1b.
	1c.
2.	2a.
	2b.
	2c.
3.	3a.
	3b.
	3c.

When Should I Do It? (My Time)

How I will find *kairos* in the chaos of my *chronos* to accomplish my goals . . .

....

....

....

....

....

....

Destination

How Will I Finish? (My Legacy)

- The legacy I hope to leave in _____ is . . .

....

....

- The legacy I hope to leave in _____ is . . .

....

....

- The legacy I hope to leave in _____ is . . .

....

....

- The legacy I hope to leave in _____ is . . .

- The legacy I hope to leave in _____ is . . .

- The legacy I hope to leave in _____ is . . .

NOTE: An electronic version of The Deeper Life Summary
is available at www.strategicrenewal.com/8Qcoaching.

Notes

Introduction

1. Robin Wauters, "Apple: 100 Million Downloads From Mac App Store in Less Than One Year," TechCrunch, December 12, 2011, http://techcrunch.com/2011/12/12/apple-500000-apps-in-mac-app-store-100-million-downloads-to-date/.

2. Cited in Don Tapsott, *Grown Up Digital* (New York: McGraw-Hill, 2009), 108–109.

3. *Merriam-Webster,* http://www.merriam-webster.com/medical/compart mentalization.

Chapter 1: Who Is God?

1. Data from The Religious Identification Survey 2008, presented in *USA Today*, March 9, 2009, http://usatoday30.usatoday.com/news/religion/2009-03-09-ARIS-faith-survey_N.htm.

2. G. Campbell Morgan sermon excerpt, presented at http://churchwarnings.blogspot.com/2010/06/idols-and-lost-vision-of-god.html.

3. A. W. Tozer, *The Knowledge of the Holy* (San Francisco: HarperCollins, 1961), 4.

4. G. Campbell Morgan, *Studies in the Prophecy of Jeremiah* (Eugene, OR: Wipf & Stock, 2010), 73.

5. A. W. Tozer, *The Pursuit of God* (Camp Hill, PA: Christian Publications, 2002), 5.

6. Tim Stafford, *Knowing the Face of God* (Grand Rapids, MI: Zondervan, 1986), 25.

7. Lee Strobel (quoting Guillermo Gonzalez and Jay W. Richards), *The Case for a Creator* (Grand Rapids, MI: Zondervan, 2004), 164.

8. A. W. Tozer, *The Pursuit of God* (Camp Hill, PA: Christian Publications, 2002), 2.

9. Quote attributed to Dawson Trotman, founder of The Navigators ministry.

10. Frederick W. Faber, "Oh, How the Thought of God Attracts." Hymn in public domain.

Chapter 2: Who Am I?

1. Quoted by Robert McGee, *The Search for Significance* (Houston: Rapha Publishing, 1990), 14.

2. Mark Batterson, *Soulprint* (Portland, OR: Multnomah, 2011), 2.

3. Leslie Cowie, "How Does Maintaining an Online Identity Affect Adolescent Identity Formation?" April 19, 2010, http://lcowie.wordpress.com/2010/04/29/social-medias-influence-on-adolescent-identity/.

4. Batterson, *Soulprint*, 3.

5. David Needham, *Birthright* (Portland, OR: Multnomah, 1979), 81.

6. Bill Gillham, *Lifetime Guarantee* (Eugene, OR: Harvest House, 1993), 72.

7. Needham, *Birthright*, 25.

8. Batterson, *Soulprint*, 2.

9. I am indebted to Pastor Rick Warren, Saddleback Church, Mission Viejo, California, for clarifying many of these concepts through his SHAPE acrostic.

10. Several sources credit this tale to Dr. James Aggrey (1875–1927), a respected educator and pastor who was born in modern-day Ghana, West Africa.

Chapter 3: Why Am I Here?

1. Melissa Dahl, "Millennials Are the Most Stressed-Out Generation, New Survey Finds," NBC News, February 7, 2013, http://www.nbcnews.com/health/millennials-are-most-stressed-out-generation-new-survey-finds-1B8296642.

2. Quoted in *Hugo* (Paramount Pictures, 2011).

3. Ibid.

4. Myles Monroe, *In Pursuit of Purpose* (Shippensburg, PA: Destiny Image Publishers, 1992), vii.

5. Statistic from Richard Vedder, director of the Center for College Affordability and Productivity, as reported by Lauren Weber, "Do Too Many Young People Go to College?" *Wall Street Journal*, June 21, 2012, http://online.wsj.com/article/SB10001424052970203960804577239253121093694.html.

6. Maddie Spielman blog, April 10, 2012, http://maddiespielman.wordpress.com/2012/04/10/whats-my-story/.

7. Chris Spielman, *That's Why I'm Here* (Grand Rapids, MI: Zondervan, 2012), 9–10.

8. Richard Bach, as quoted in Peter McWilliams, *Do It! Let's Get Off Our Buts* (New York: Bantam, 1991), 144.

9. Definition of *purpose* found at http://dictionary.reference.com/browse/purpose.

Chapter 4: What Really Matters?

1. The Barna Group, "Americans Are Most Likely to Base Truth on Feelings," February 12, 2002, http://www.barna.org/barna-update/article/5-barna-update/67-americans-are-most-likely-to-base-truth-on-feelings.

2. Ronald Reagan, cited by Linda and Richard Byre in *Teaching Your Children Values* (New York: Simon & Schuster, 1993), 12.

3. George W. Bush, *A Charge to Keep* (New York: HarperCollins, 2001), 25.

4. Chris Spielman, *That's Why I'm Here* (Grand Rapids, MI: Zondervan, 2012), 26.

5. Ibid., 33.

6. Watchman Nee, *Not I But Christ* (New York: Christian Fellowship, 1974), 64.

7. Gordon MacDonald, "Mastering Ministry" conference, January 1993.

8. Tony Campolo presentation, "If I Had It to Live Over Again," https://soundcloud.com/tonycampolo/if-i-had-it-to-live-over-again.

9. Malcolm Forbes with Jeff Bloch, *What Happened to Their Kids?* (New York: Simon & Schuster, 1990), 237–239.

Chapter 5: What Shall I Do?

1. Bernard Baruch, as quoted by Charles Swindoll in *Come Before Winter* (Portland, OR: Multnomah, 1985), 23.
2. John Maxwell, *Developing the Leader Within You* (Nashville: Thomas Nelson, 1993), 20.
3. Stephen Covey, *First Things First* (New York: Simon & Schuster, 1994), 39.
4. William Cook, *Success, Motivation, and the Scriptures* (Nashville: Broadman, 1974), 127.
5. E. C. McKenzie, *Mac's Giant Book of Quips and Quotes* (Eugene, OR: Harvest House, 1980), 76.
6. Cited by Maxwell in *Developing the Leader Within You*, 28.
7. Ibid., 25–26.
8. Youth Sports Statistics, cited at Statistic Brain, drawn from Minnesota Amateur Sports Commission, Athletic Footwear Association, *USA Today* survey, and Michigan State University, http://www.statisticbrain.com/youth-sports-statistics/.
9. E. J. Dionne Jr., "Clinton Swipes the GOP's Lyrics; The Democrat as Liberal Republican," *Washington Post*, July 21, 1996, C1.
10. Survey findings quoted by Chris Wagner, "Pressure Points," Center for Parent/Youth Understanding, http://www.cpyu.org/Page.aspx?id=77250.
11. Lysa TerKeurst, "I Don't Want to Raise Successful Children," November 19, 2009, http://www.proverbs31.org/devotions/i-dont-want-to-raise-successful-children-2009-11/.
12. Wayne Martindale and Jerry Root, eds., *The Quotable Lewis* (Wheaton, IL: Tyndale House, 1989), 496.

Chapter 6: How Shall I Do It?

1. Carlos Vargas, *Dreams Are Cheap* (Guatemala: Punto Creativo, 2013), 85.
2. Unattributed story presented in a variety of sources, including *Discipleshape* by Dan R. Crawford (Peabody, MA: Hendrickson, 1998), Week Two, n.p.
3. Adapted from John Maxwell, *Be All You Can Be* (Wheaton, IL: Victor Books, 1987), 68.
4. African folklore, as told by Dan Montano, "Lions or Gazelles?" *The Economist*, July 6, 1985, 37.
5. Tom Morris, *True Success* (New York: Putnam, 1994), 217.
6. Ibid., 217–218.
7. Anna Chiu, "Olympic Winner Has the Golden Touch," April 8, 2013, *Free Press*, University of Southern Maine, http://usmfreepress.org/2013/04/08/olympic-winner-has-the-golden-touch/.
8. Adapted from John Maxwell, *Be All You Can Be* (Wheaton, IL: Victor Books, 1987), 61.
9. Ibid., 62.
10. Richard Leyda, "Henrietta Cornelia Mears," Talbot School of Theology, Biola University, http://www.talbot.edu/ce20/educators/protestant/henrietta_mears/.

Chapter 7: When Shall I Do It?

1. Laura Petrecca, "All Work and No Play?" as quoted in *USA Today*, March 7, 2013, http://www.usatoday.com/story/news/nation/2013/03/06/mobile-workforce-all-work/1958673/.

2. Ibid.

3. Richard Swenson, *Margin* (Colorado Springs: NavPress, 1992), 145.

4. Elisabeth Elliot, *Discipline* (Grand Rapids, MI: Baker, 1982), 97.

5. Quoted by Daniel J. Boorstein in *The Discoverers* (New York: Random House, 1983), 25.

6. E. F. Shumacher, *Good Work* (New York: Harper & Row, 1979), 25.

7. Swenson, *Margin*, 153.

8. Charles Swindoll, *The Quest for Character* (Portland, OR: Multnomah, 1987), 119–124.

9. John MacArthur, *New Testament Commentary on Ephesians* (Chicago: Moody, 1986), 222.

10. Wendy Cole, "Please, Go Away," *Time* Magazine, October 11, 2004, http://content.time.com/time/magazine/article/0,9171,995299,00.html.

11. Betty Lin-Fisher, "Office Distractions Make Getting the Job Done Difficult," *Houston Chronicle*, February 27, 2006, http://www.chron.com/business/article/Office-distractions-make-getting-the-job-done-1663366.php.

12. Louise Story, "Anywhere the Eye Can See, It's Likely to See an Ad," *New York Times*, January 15, 2007, http://www.nytimes.com/2007/01/15/business/media/15everywhere.html.

13. Nielsen, "The Social Media Report, 2012," http://www.nielsen.com/us/en/newswire/2012/social-media-report-2012-social-media-comes-of-age.html.

14. Joe Queenan, "Lack of Sleep Costs Billions? How About Cats?" *Wall Street Journal*, January 25, 2013, http://online.wsj.com/article/SB10001424127887324039504578260150922545678.html.

15. Sue Shellenbarger, "More Work Goes 'Undercover'," *Wall Street Journal*, November 14, 2012, http://online.wsj.com/article/SB1000142412788732355100457816922977737046.html.

16. Jill Briscoe, *Before You Say Amen* (Colorado Springs: David C. Cook, 1989), 15.

17. Del Fehsenfeld Jr., *Spirit of Revival* magazine, Life Action Ministries: November 1986), 2.

Chapter 8: How Will I Finish?

1. UNICEF, *The State of the World's Children 2009: Maternal and Newborn Health*, www.unicef.org/sowc09/report/report.php.

2. Food and Agriculture Organization for the United Nations, *The State of Food Insecurity in the World (2009)*, 2, ftp://ftp.fao.org/docrep/fao/012/i0876e/i0876e.pdf.

3. UNICEF, *The State of the World's Children 2007: Women and Children*, 5, www.unicef.org/sowc07/docs/sowc07.pdf.

4. Anup Shah, "Today, Around 21,000 Children Died Around the World," *Global Issues*, September 24, 2011, http://www.globalissues.org/article/715/today-21000-children-died-around-the-world.

5. Percentage of churchgoers in 2004, as quoted by Rebecca Barnes and Lindy Lowry, "7 Startling Facts: An Up-Close Look at Church Attendance in America," http://www.churchleaders.com/pastors/pastor-articles/139575-7-startling-facts-an-up-close-look-at-church-attendance-in-america.html.

6. John. S. Dickerson, *The Great Evangelical Recession* (Grand Rapids, MI: Baker, 2013), 22.

7. Data from The Religious Identification Survey 2008, presented in *USA Today*, March 9, 2009, http://usatoday30.usatoday.com/news/religion/2009-03-09-ARIS-faith-survey_N.htm.

8. Rebekah Montgomery, quoting a Focus on the Family report, "Pastors and Wives at the Breaking Point," *Adventist Review*, http://www.adventistreview.org/article/680/archives/issue-2006–1522/pastors-and-wives-at-the-breaking-point.

9. Clifton Daniel, ed., "Billionaire J. Paul Getty Dies in Britain," *Chronicle of the 20th Century* (Liberty, MO: JL International Publishing, 1992), 1110.

10. History Channel, "Billionaire's Kidnapped Grandson Found in Italy, December 15, 1973, http://www.history.com/this-day-in-history/billionaires-kidnapped-grandson-found-in-italy.

11. "Billionaire Getty Dies," Associated Press article, May 7, 2003, http://usatoday30.usatoday.com/money/2003-04-17-getty-obit_x.htm.

12. Billy Graham, *Nearing Home* (Nashville: Thomas Nelson, 2011), 42.

13. Fred Barlow, *Profiles in Evangelism: David Brainerd* (Murfreesboro, TN: Sword of the Lord, 1976), reprinted at http://www.wholesomewords.org/missions/biobrain.html.

Epilogue

1. Wayne Martindale and Jerry Root, eds., *The Quotable Lewis* (Wheaton, IL: Tyndale, 1989), 241.

2. Richard S. Halverson, quoted by Daryl Witmer, "As Time Goes On, You Become Your Choices," *Bangor Daily News*, February 3, 2007, http://archive.bangordailynews.com/2007/02/03/as-time-goes-on-you-become-your-choices/.

Appendix 13: Quick Tips on Time Management

1. C. S. Lewis, *The Screwtape Letters* (New York: HarperCollins, reprint ed. 2001).

About the Authors

For three decades **Daniel Henderson** has been guiding individuals, leaders, and churches to embrace experiences of powerful spiritual renewal. He has served as a senior pastor to thousands in congregations in California and Minnesota. Today he speaks across the nation at leadership conferences and local churches while coaching pastors and business leaders in the principles of a strategic and spiritually significant life. He is a husband, father, grandfather, and author of eight books. For more information about his ministry, visit www.strategicrenewal.com and www.64fellowship.com.

Brenda Brown has been teaching on principles of purposeful living for twenty-five years. As a life coach, retreat speaker, and women's ministry leader, Brenda encourages mothers to pursue a life of influence and raise their children without regrets. For more information on coaching for moms on *The Deeper Life,* visit www.strategic renewal.com/8Qcoaching.

Take Your Prayer Life From Ordinary to Extraordinary

It's no wonder so many people are discouraged with prayer. Instead of a genuine encounter with God, prayer is often limited to a grocery list of requests. Maybe you, too, seek God's hand rather than His face.

How do you truly connect with God through prayer? Renewal leader and pastor Daniel Henderson has helped innumerable Christians transform their prayer life. In this book, he shows you how to:

- Overcome common barriers to praying effectively
- Awaken your prayer life with simple, biblical patterns of prayer
- Enjoy Spirit-led prayer sparked by Scripture passages

When you experience the profound difference of worship-based prayer, your faith and life will never be the same.

Transforming Prayer by Daniel Henderson

BETHANYHOUSE

Stay up-to-date on your favorite books and authors with our free e-newsletters. Sign up today at bethanyhouse.com.

Find us on Facebook. facebook.com/BHPnonfiction

Follow us on Twitter. @bethany_house